overcoming anxious attachment

CONQUER FEAR OF ABANDONMENT, ELIMINATE RELATIONSHIP ANXIETY, EFFECTIVELY COMMUNICATE YOUR FEELINGS, AND ACHIEVE EMOTIONAL FREEDOM

KELLY ANNE PETTY

table of contents

introduction

In the heart of human existence lies a profound longing—a desire for deep, meaningful connections that nurture our souls and secure our place in the world. Yet, for many, this yearning is shadowed by a pervasive fear of abandonment, a whispering apprehension that the love and security we crave might slip through our fingers. You're not alone if you've ever felt this fear or caught yourself in the web of anxious attachment. I deeply and personally understand the courage it takes to confront these fears. And I welcome you to this journey from this place of understanding and compassion.

My name is Kelly Anne Petty, and I have dedicated my life to exploring the depths of human emotion and the pathways to healing. My professional journey began in the field of psychotherapy, where I immersed myself in the challenging yet rewarding world of addiction treatment and hospice care. These experiences taught me the power of empathy, the importance of holistic well-being approaches, and the transformative potential of genuinely connecting with others at a soulful level. Driven by a passion for holistic healing, I expanded my practice to include massage therapy and CranioSacral therapy, further deepening my understanding of the intricate links between mind, body, and spirit.

"Overcoming Anxious Attachment - Transforming Insecurity Into Confidence" is born from a heartfelt desire to share the insights and tools I've gathered over years of personal and professional exploration. This book guides you from the shadows of fear and insecurity to a place of emotional freedom and confidence. Together, we will navigate the complexities of anxious attachment, learning to understand its roots, clearly communicate our needs, and build relationships grounded in trust and mutual respect.

Our conversation will be warm and supportive, akin to a therapeutic session or a heart-to-heart with a trusted friend. I believe in approaching sensitive topics with an open heart and a non-judgmental mind, creating a safe space for vulnerability and growth. This book stands apart for its blend of professional insight, personal compassion, and practical, holistic strategies. Through a combination of theoretical understanding, personal anecdotes, practical exercises, and the latest research, we will embark on a comprehensive journey toward healing.

Let me share a brief moment from my practice that continues to inspire me: I once worked with an individual who felt perpetually trapped by their fears of abandonment, believing they were unworthy of love. Through our journey together, they slowly began to peel away the layers of insecurity, learning to stand in their truth and embrace their inherent worth. Witnessing their transformation was a profound reminder of the power each of us holds to rewrite our stories.

This book is structured into five parts, each designed to build upon the last, guiding you through understanding anxious attachment, confronting and transforming it, and finally, living with a sense of security and confidence in your relationships. I invite you to engage with this book actively through reflection, journaling, and applying the strategies to your life. Your participation is vital to turning insight into transformation.

Thank you for your trust and willingness to embark on this journey. While the path may present challenges, deeper connection and self-discovery rewards are immeasurable. Together, we can move toward a future where fear no longer dictates our relationships and confidence in our worth defines us. Here's to a journey of healing, growth, and profound transformation.

the roots of attachment: exploring bowlby and ainsworth's legacy

Within the tapestry of human emotions and relationships, attachment stands out as a crucial thread, weaving through our interactions and shaping our connections from the cradle to the grave. Understanding attachment, its origins, and its profound impact on our lives is not just an academic endeavor; it's a key to unlocking the doors to our emotional worlds, making sense of our behaviors, and, most importantly, navigating the complexities of our relationships.

In the dimly lit rooms of post-war England, two pioneers, John Bowlby and Mary Ainsworth, embarked on a quest to explore the unseen bonds that tie children to their caregivers. Their groundbreaking work not only altered the landscape of developmental psychology but also offered a new lens through which to view our emotional lives. This chapter peels back the layers of their discoveries, laying bare the foundations of attachment theory and its relevance to our everyday lives.

FOUNDATIONAL THEORIES

In the aftermath of World War II, John Bowlby, a British psychoanalyst, observed the profound distress experienced by children separated from their parents. This observation led him to challenge the prevailing psychoanalytic theories of the time, proposing instead that these reactions were biologically programmed responses essential for survival. Bowlby's theory suggests that children are born with an innate drive to form attachments with caregivers to protect them from threats. This idea, revolutionary at the time, laid the groundwork for what would later become known as attachment theory.

Mary Ainsworth, an American-Canadian developmental psychologist, joined forces with Bowlby, bringing her meticulous research methodologies to bear on the study of attachment. Through detailed observations of mother-child interactions, Ainsworth's work in Uganda and Baltimore provided empirical evidence supporting and expanding Bowlby's theoretical framework. Her contributions were instrumental in moving attachment theory from an abstract hypothesis to a scientifically validated model of human development.

Secure Base and Safe Haven

The "secure base" concept is central to Bowlby's theory—a caregiver provides a foundation of security from which the child can explore the world. The child returns to this haven for comfort and reassurance when faced with unfamiliar or challenging situations. A secure base is crucial for healthy emotional and social development, enabling children to venture confidently, knowing they have a safe place of retreat.

Ainsworth's "Strange Situation" experiment, a structured observational study, brought the secure base concept to life. By observing how infants reacted to being briefly separated from their care-givers and reunited, Ainsworth identified distinct patterns of attachment behaviors. These findings underscored the importance of the caregiver's responsiveness to the child's needs in fostering a sense of security and trust.

Evolutionary Perspective

Bowlby's attachment theory was grounded in an evolutionary perspective, positing that attachment behaviors are part of a survival strategy. From this viewpoint, the emotional bonds between caregiver and child are not just social constructs but have deep roots in our evolutionary past, designed to ensure the offspring's survival until they reach maturity. This perspective highlights the adaptive nature of attachment behaviors, showing how they have been shaped by natural selection to enhance the chances of survival.

Attachment Styles Conceptualization

Drawing on Bowlby's and Ainsworth's foundational work, attach-ment styles were developed to categorize how individuals relate to others in close relationships. Ainsworth's observations identified three primary attachment styles: secure, anxious-preoccupied, and dismissive-avoidant, with a fourth style, fearful-avoidant, added later by other researchers.

- Secure attachment is characterized by comfort with intimacy and independence, resulting from consistent and responsive caregiving.
- Anxious-preoccupied attachment emerges from inconsistent caregiving, leading to anxiety about the caregiver's availability and preoccupation with the relationship.

- Dismissive-avoidant attachment is marked by a detachment from the caregiver and focusing on self-sufficiency, often as a defense against rejection.
- Fearful-avoidant attachment combines features of anxious and avoidant styles, with individuals often feeling torn between the desire for closeness and the fear of getting hurt.

These attachment styles, conceptualized through Ainsworth's work, provide a framework for understanding the complex dynamics of human relationships, extending beyond the caregiver-child dyad to adult romantic partnerships.

Amid our bustling daily lives, we seldom consider the invisible threads of attachment that shape our interactions and emotional landscapes. Yet, understanding these bonds and the attachment styles we've developed over time can offer profound insights into our relationship patterns, emotional responses, and how we navigate our world. Whether secure, anxiously attached, dismissive, or fearful, each style reflects a strategy for dealing with closeness and distance, shaped by our earliest experiences with those who cared for us.

1.2 ANXIOUS ATTACHMENT UNVEILED: CHARACTERISTICS AND ORIGINS

In the landscape of attachment styles, anxious attachment emerges as a complex pattern marked by a deep-seated fear of abandonment and an insatiable need for reassurance. This style is not merely a list of behaviors but a reflection of the intricate dance between past experiences and present fears, profoundly influencing how individuals navigate their relationships.

Defining Anxious Attachment

At the heart of anxious attachment is a paradoxical blend of longing for closeness and the dread of not being enough to keep that closeness intact. Characteristics that define this attachment style include:

- A pervasive fear of abandonment, often manifesting as vigilance toward any signs that a loved one might leave.
- A continuous need for reassurance from partners or friends, seeking validation that the relationship is secure.
- An acute sensitivity to the moods and behaviors of others, interpreting them as indicators of the relationship's health.
- A tendency toward emotional highs and lows is based on the attachment figure's perceived availability.

These traits, while protective, often lead to a self-amplifying cycle of anxiety and dependence in relationships, where the more one fears loss, the more one clings, inadvertently straining the very connections one hopes to strengthen.

Developmental Origins

The roots of anxious attachment stretch back to the cradle, where the interplay of presence and absence shapes the infant's worldview. Inconsistent caregiving, where warmth and responsiveness are unpredictably interspersed with neglect or indifference, lays the groundwork for anxious attachment. This inconsistency leaves the child in a state of confusion and insecurity, unsure of whether their needs will be met or ignored, fostering a chronic sense of anxiety about their worth and the reliability of their caregivers.

This early template for relationships teaches that love and attention are conditional and unpredictable, leading individuals to grow vigilant and doubtful about the stability of their bonds with others. The child learns to associate love with anxiety, a lesson carried into adult relationships.

Impact on Adult Relationships

The anxious attachment style profoundly influences how individuals perceive and react within adult relationships. This impact manifests in several ways:

- Heightened relationship anxiety, where every minor conflict or shift in dynamics is seen through the lens of potential abandonment.
- An over-reliance on partners for emotional validation often places an undue burden on the relationship to fulfill unmet childhood needs.
- Difficulty in trusting partners' affections and intentions, leading to cycles of doubt and reassurance-seeking behaviors.
- A propensity to remain in less-than-fulfilling or harmful relationships out of fear of being alone.

These patterns, deeply ingrained, can make relationships feel like a rollercoaster of emotions, with intense fears of loss overshadowing moments of genuine connection.

The Role of Self-Perception

Central to understanding anxious attachment is recognizing how self-perception, shaped by early experiences of inconsistency and conditional acceptance, influences relationship behaviors. Individuals with anxious attachment often harbor deep-seated beliefs of unworthiness, fearing that they are inherently flawed and, therefore, unlovable. This fear drives a constant search for external validation, with every interaction serving as a litmus test for their worth in the eyes of their loved ones.

This skewed self-perception leads to a self-fulfilling prophecy, where the fear of rejection prompts behaviors that strain relationships, reinforcing the belief in one's unworthiness. The challenge then becomes not just about managing external relationships but about healing the relationship with oneself, recognizing that the path to security lies in rewriting these internal narratives of unworthiness and embracing one's inherent value.

In the tapestry of human connections, anxious attachment embodies the delicate balance between desire and fear, closeness, and the dread of its loss. Understanding this attachment style's characteristics, origins, and impacts opens the door to compassionate self-awareness and the possibility of growth. It highlights the importance of nurturing our relationships with others and, crucially, our relationship with ourselves. Through this understanding, we can unravel the knots of fear and longing, stepping into a space where love is not a source of anxiety but a wellspring of strength and confidence.

1.3 THE BRAIN ON ATTACHMENT: NEUROLOGICAL UNDERPINNINGS OF ANXIOUS ATTACHMENT

The intricate dance of attachment is choreographed in the early years of our lives and deeply engraved in our brains' neural pathways. As we peel away the layers of anxious attachment, it becomes crucial to understand the biological framework that underlies these emotional landscapes. This exploration leads us into neuroscience, where recent advancements have begun to illuminate the neural correlates of attachment styles, offering fresh insights into how our brains shape—and are shaped by—our attachment experiences.

Brain Structures and Attachment

At the core of the brain's attachment network lie several vital structures, each playing a pivotal role in emotion regulation and response to attachment-related stimuli. Two of the most significant are the amygdala and the prefrontal cortex, which form a complex system governing our reactions to perceived threats and safety cues in relationships.

- The amygdala, often called the brain's alarm system, is central to processing emotions, especially fear and anxiety. In the context of anxious attachment, the amygdala's heightened vigilance for signs of rejection or abandonment can lead to an amplified response to even minor relationship stressors.
- The prefrontal cortex is the brain's executive center, regulating emotions and impulses. It helps modulate the amygdala's reactivity, calming fears and fostering emotional resilience. However, in individuals with anxious attachment, this regulation can be less effective, leading to increased anxiety and emotional dysregulation.

Together, these structures form a dynamic interplay where the balance between emotional reactivity and regulation shapes our attachment behaviors and experiences.

Stress Response Mechanisms

Individuals with anxious attachment often exhibit a heightened stress response, a legacy of early experiences where the unpredictability of caregiver availability left them in a perpetual state of alertness. This state of hyperarousal activates the body's stress response system, leading to the release of stress hormones such as cortisol.

- In moments perceived as threatening to the relationship, the body's fight or flight response is triggered, preparing the individual to either cling tighter to maintain closeness or to prepare for emotional pain. This response, while adaptive in genuinely threatening situations, can become maladaptive in the context of everyday relationship dynamics, intensifying feelings of anxiety and insecurity.

Neuroplasticity and Healing

Amid the challenges presented by anxious attachment, the concept of neuroplasticity emerges as a beacon of hope. Neuroplasticity is the brain's remarkable ability to reorganize and form new neural connections throughout life. This capacity for change means that the patterns of thought and behavior associated with anxious attachment are not set in stone; they can be reshaped through targeted therapeutic interventions and experiences.

- Engaging in practices that foster secure attachment experiences and emotional regulation, such as mindfulness, therapy, and secure relationship dynamics, can gradually rewire the brain's response to attachment cues. Over time, these new pathways can diminish the intensity of the stress response and enhance the effectiveness of emotional regulation strategies, paving the way for more secure attachment patterns to emerge.

Research Findings

A growing body of research has begun to map the neurological patterns associated with anxious attachment, shedding light on the biological underpinnings of this complex attachment style. Studies utilizing functional magnetic resonance imaging (fMRI) have revealed distinct patterns of brain activity in individuals with anxious attachment, particularly in response to attachment-related stimuli.

- One key finding is the increased activation of the amygdala in response to cues perceived as threatening to the attachment bond, such as images or scenarios depicting rejection or abandonment. This heightened reactivity underscores the role of the amygdala in the fear and anxiety characteristic of anxious attachment.
- Conversely, research has also highlighted differences in prefrontal cortex activation, suggesting that individuals with anxious attachment may have difficulty engaging the neural circuits involved in emotion regulation. This difficulty underscores the challenges faced in managing the intense emotions that arise in close relationships.

These findings not only validate the lived experiences of those with anxious attachment but also point toward targeted interventions that can address the specific neural pathways involved. Understanding the brain's role in attachment opens the door to more effective strategies for healing and growth, offering individuals a path toward transforming their attachment patterns and fostering healthier, more fulfilling relationships.

As we delve deeper into the neuroscience of attachment, we uncover the profound ways in which our brains are shaped by our earliest relationships and how, in turn, these neural patterns shape our experiences of love and connection. This exploration not only enriches our understanding of anxious attachment but also highlights the incredible adaptability of the human brain, offering hope for change and healing. The journey through the neurological underpinnings of attachment reveals a landscape where past patterns do not dictate future possibilities; instead, they pave the way for growth, transformation, and the continuous reshaping of our emotional worlds.

1.4 DECODING YOUR ATTACHMENT STYLE: SELF-ASSESSMENT TOOLS

Gaining insight into our attachment style opens doors to understanding how we relate to others, providing a map to navigate the complexities of our emotions and relationships. This self-awareness is the first step in addressing patterns hindering our ability to form secure and fulfilling connections.

Importance of Self-Knowledge

Knowing our attachment style isn't just about labeling ourselves; it's about unlocking a deeper understanding of our relationship needs, fears, and behaviors. This awareness is crucial for personal growth and cultivating healthier relationships. It allows us to recognize why we react the way we do in certain situations, guiding us toward more adaptive coping strategies and communication patterns. Armed with this knowledge, we can make conscious choices about engaging with others and address the root causes of our relational challenges.

Questionnaires and Quizzes

Various self-assessment tools are available to help individuals pinpoint their attachment style. These tools range from questionnaires found in psychological texts and online platforms to quizzes developed by relationship experts. They typically include scenarios and reactions that one might have in a relationship, asking you to rate how much you agree or disagree with each response. While these tools provide a good starting point, it's essential to approach them with an open mind and see them as a guide rather than a definitive answer. Each person's attachment experience is unique, and these tools should catalyze deeper reflection, not as a box that defines us.

- Attachment Style Questionnaire (ASQ): This tool assesses adult attachment styles across dimensions such as confidence, discomfort with closeness, and relationships as secondary.
- Experiences in Close Relationships-Revised (ECR-R) Questionnaire: A widely used self-reporting tool that measures adult attachment dimensions of anxiety and avoidance.

Engaging with these questionnaires can spark insights into how you approach relationships, highlighting tendencies towards anxiety, avoidance, or comfort with intimacy.

Reflective Practices

Beyond questionnaires and quizzes, engaging in reflective practices offers a more nuanced exploration of our attachment patterns. Journaling, in particular, provides a private space to observe and note our behaviors, thoughts, and emotions as they unfold in our relationships. Here are some prompts to get started:

- Reflect on a recent conflict in a relationship. What emotions did you feel? How did you respond to those emotions?
- Think about a time when you felt particularly secure or insecure in a relationship. What contributed to those feelings?
- Consider your reactions to separations or reunions. Do you find yourself preoccupied with the thought of being left, or do you strive for independence?

These reflections help reveal patterns and themes in our behavior, guiding us toward a more profound understanding of our attachment style.

Professional Assessment

While self-assessment tools and reflective practices provide valuable insights, consulting with a professional offers a more comprehensive understanding of one's attachment style and the underlying issues that may contribute to it. Psychologists and therapists trained in attachment theory can help interpret the nuances of your responses and behaviors, providing a more tailored analysis. Moreover, they can offer guidance on therapeutic approaches and strategies to address challenges related to your attachment style.

Seeking professional assessment becomes particularly valuable when anxious attachment patterns significantly impact your quality of life and relationships. A therapist can help untangle the web of past experiences that contribute to current attachment behaviors, fostering a journey toward healing and growth. They can also support the development of secure attachment strategies, enhancing emotional regulation, self-esteem, and the ability to form healthy relationships.

Recognizing our attachment style through self-assessment tools, reflective practices, and professional guidance marks a critical step in understanding ourselves better and improving our relationships. This discovery process sheds light on why we interact the way we do with those closest to us and opens pathways to change, growth, and deeper connection. By embracing this exploration with curiosity and openness, we set the stage for transforming our relationship approach, moving towards more secure and fulfilling connections.

1.5 THE SPECTRUM OF ATTACHMENT: NAVIGATING BETWEEN SECURE AND INSECURE

The idea of attachment styles as rigid, unchangeable categories can be a limiting way to view our complex emotional landscapes. Recognizing that these styles exist more accurately on a spectrum allows a more fluid understanding of our relationship behaviors and needs. This perspective acknowledges the nuanced realities of human attachment, opening up possibilities for growth and change.

Continuum of Attachment

Rather than being fixed points, attachment styles ebb and flow across a spectrum influenced by many factors, including life experiences, relationship dynamics, and personal growth efforts. This spectrum ranges from secure to insecure, with anxious, avoidant, and disorganized attachment serving as waypoints rather than destinations. Understanding attachment as a spectrum reinforces that our attachment style is not a life sentence but a starting point from which we can move towards greater security and fulfillment in our relationships.

Flexibility of Attachment Styles

The fluid nature of attachment is evident in how individuals display different attachment behaviors across various relationships and contexts. For example, someone might exhibit secure attachment traits with close friends but anxious attachment behaviors in romantic relationships. This variability challenges the idea of static attachment styles, highlighting how our interactions and the specific dynamics of each relationship can influence our attachment behaviors. It's a reminder that our capacity for change and adaptation extends to our relational worlds, making the towards secure attachment a dynamic and ongoing process.

- Different behaviors in various relationships: Reflecting on how you act with family versus friends can reveal the flexibility of your attachment style.
- Contextual influences: Considering how stress, life transitions, and other external factors temporarily alter your attachment behaviors can help you understand this flexibility.

Path to Secure Attachment

Moving towards secure attachment involves acknowledging the spectrum of attachment and recognizing where we currently fall on it. From this place of awareness, we can embark on a path defined by personal development and healing. This path includes:

- Self-awareness: Understanding your attachment patterns, triggers, and needs is the first step toward change. This understanding may involve reflecting on past relationships and upbringing to identify the origins of your attachment style.
- Emotion regulation: Managing one's emotional responses is crucial, especially in situations that trigger insecurity or fear of abandonment. Practices such as mindfulness and deep breathing can be helpful tools.
- Building self-esteem: Working on your self-worth independent of external validation supports the development of secure attachment by reducing reliance on others for feelings of adequacy.
- Seeking therapeutic support: Engaging with a knowledgeable therapist can provide guidance and

support as you work through attachment-related issues and strive toward security.

- Cultivating secure relationships: Surrounding yourself with consistent, reliable, and emotionally responsive relationships can reinforce feelings of security and belonging.

The journey towards secure attachment is not linear but involves cycles of learning, growth, setbacks, and successes. Patience, compassion for oneself, and persistence are fundamental companions on this path.

The Role of Relationships

Both platonic and romantic relationships play a significant role in transforming insecure attachment patterns. Healthy, supportive relationships act as mirrors, reflecting our worth and helping to repair breaches in our sense of belonging and security. These relationships offer opportunities for experiencing consistency, reliability, and emotional responsiveness—core components of secure attachment.

- Modeling secure behaviors: Engaging with individuals who embody secure attachment can provide a template for healthy relational behaviors, contrasting previously learned patterns.
- Emotional co-regulation: Healthy relationships provide a context for learning how to regulate emotions in the presence of others, a critical skill for those with insecure attachment styles.
- Corrective experiences: Positive relational experiences serve as corrective emotional experiences, challenging old beliefs about unworthiness and abandonment. Over time, these experiences can rewire our expectations and

reactions in relationships, moving us closer to secure attachment.

The transformative power of relationships underscores the importance of choosing connections that nourish and support our growth. It highlights how our journey towards secure attachment is intertwined with the quality of our interactions and the relational environments we cultivate.

Navigating the attachment spectrum requires a nuanced understanding of the fluidity of our attachment styles and the recognition that growth and change are always within reach. By embracing the flexibility of our attachment behaviors, committing to personal development, and fostering healthy relationships, we can move towards greater security and fulfillment in our connections. The path toward secure attachment is an individual and relational endeavor rooted in the belief that transformation is possible through awareness, effort, and supportive connections.

the seeds of attachment: from early bonds to adult relationships

I magine a tree's branches reaching confidently towards the sky, its leaves rustling softly in the breeze. Now, consider its roots, hidden beneath the surface, grounding and nourishing it. Our attachment styles are much like these roots, invisible but fundamentally shaping the way we grow and interact with the world around us. In this chapter, we delve into the genesis and evolution of anxious attachment, tracing its development from the earliest interactions in infancy to its manifestation in adult relationships.

Early Interactions

The dance between a caregiver and their infant sets the stage for the child's emotional and relational blueprint. A foundation of trust and security is laid when a baby cries and a caregiver responds with warmth and consistency. Picture the countless moments of feeding, comforting, and playing in the first months of life. These are not just routine caregiving tasks but the building blocks of attachment. However, when responses from caregivers are unpredictable or absent, the seeds of anxious attachment begin to take root. The infant learns that the world is not always a reliable source of comfort, leading to heightened anxiety and a desperate need for closeness to ensure survival.

- Responsive Care: Regular, predictable care, where caregivers warmly meet an infant's needs, fosters a sense of security.
- Inconsistency and Neglect: On the flip side, inconsistency or neglect instills a sense of uncertainty and fear, contributing to the development of anxious attachment.

Critical Periods

Research highlights specific windows in child development, known as critical periods when the impact of caregiving interactions on attachment is particularly pronounced. The first year of life is paramount for attachment formation. During this time, the infant's brain rapidly develops, making it especially sensitive to the quality of caregiving experiences. These early experiences influence immediate behavior and impact how individuals approach relationships later in life. Recognizing these critical periods underscores the importance of nurturing and responsive care.

- First-Year Sensitivity: The brain's development in the first year makes it a critical period for establishing a secure attachment base.
- Long-Term Impact: The quality of care and interaction during critical periods has far-reaching effects on adult relationship patterns.

Longitudinal Studies

Longitudinal studies tracking individuals from infancy into adulthood provide compelling evidence of how early attachment experiences shape our relational worlds. For instance, studies following children identified as securely or insecurely attached in infancy have found that these early attachment styles can predict relational and emotional patterns years later. These studies underscore that the roots of anxious attachment, once established, tend to persist, influencing how individuals perceive and react within their adult relationships, from their choice of partners to their expectations and fears within those partnerships.

- Predictive Value: Early attachment classifications correlate with relationship dynamics and emotional health in later life.
- Continuity and Change: While early attachment styles can persist, longitudinal studies highlight the potential for change influenced by later experiences and interventions.

Personal Narratives

Reflecting on our histories can be a powerful tool for understanding the development of our attachment style. Consider the caregiving environment of your early years. Were your emotional needs consistently met with understanding and warmth, or did you often feel alone and unheard? Understanding these early chapters of our lives can shed light on the patterns we carry into our adult relationships. Here are some prompts to guide your reflection:

- Think about a moment from your childhood when you felt scared or upset. How did your caregivers respond?
- Reflect on your relationships with primary caregivers. Can you identify patterns in how they interacted with you and how you responded to them?
- Consider how these early experiences have shaped your expectations and fears in adult relationships.

You can journal these reflections, discuss them with a trusted friend, or explore them with a therapist. The goal is not to place blame but to understand and, if necessary, to heal.

As we explore the roots of anxious attachment, it becomes clear that our earliest experiences play a pivotal role in shaping how we connect with others. From the responsiveness of our caregivers to the critical periods of our development and the insights gained from longitudinal studies, a complex picture emerges. By intertwining these threads of comprehension with our personal stories, we create opportunities for growth and transformation. This exploration is not just about looking back; it's about moving forward with greater awareness and compassion toward ourselves and our relationships.

2.2 THE ROLE OF CAREGIVERS IN SHAPING ATTACHMENT

In the intricate dance of developing attachments, caregivers play a pivotal role, acting as the primary architects of the emotional environment in which a child's attachment style is nurtured. This section delves into how caregivers establish the foundation for secure or anxious attachments through their distinctive caregiving styles, emotional availability, and interventions. Moreover, we delve into the cyclical nature of attachment styles across generations, underscoring the potential for positive change.

Caregiving Styles

How caregivers interact with their children significantly influences the formation of attachment patterns. There are distinct caregiving styles, each with its impact on a child's sense of security and style of attachment:

- Consistent and Responsive: Caregivers who are consistently available and respond promptly and sensitively to a child's needs foster a sense of reliability in their relationships. This style is most conducive to developing secure attachments.
- Unpredictable and Inconsistent: When caregivers oscillate between responsiveness and neglect, children may develop anxious attachments characterized by uncertainty and a craving for constant reassurance.
- Detached and Unresponsive: Caregivers who regularly exhibit detachment or a lack of responsiveness can contribute to avoidant attachment styles in children, where they learn to self-soothe and avoid seeking comfort from others.

The style adopted by caregivers sets the stage for the initial attachment bond and models for children how relationships function, influencing their future interactions and expectations of others.

The Mirror of Emotion

Children look to their caregivers as mirrors, reflecting the emotional significance of their experiences. Caregivers' emotional availability and responsiveness are critical factors in this mirroring process, shaping a child's ability to regulate emotions and develop a sense of self-worth. When caregivers meet a child's emotional expressions with understanding and support, they validate their feelings, teaching them that their emotions are real and manageable. This mirroring process guides children toward healthy emotional self-regulation and secure attachment styles.

Conversely, when caregivers dismiss or ignore a child's emotional needs, the child may internalize a belief that their feelings are unwarranted or burdensome, contributing to anxious attachment patterns. The importance of caregivers being emotionally attuned and present, offering a responsive and supportive reflection of the child's emotional world, is highlighted in contrast to caregivers being dismissive or neglectful of the child's needs.

Interventions

Recognizing the significant influence of caregiving on attachment development, experts have developed various interventions to help caregivers nurture secure attachments, especially when they notice signs of anxious attachment patterns. These interventions often focus on enhancing caregivers' sensitivity to their children's needs and improving their emotional availability. Some effective strategies include:

- Parenting Workshops: These programs provide caregivers with the knowledge and tools to effectively understand and respond to their children's emotional cues.
- Home Visiting Programs: Trained professionals offer in-home support and guidance, helping caregivers create a nurturing and responsive caregiving environment.
- Therapeutic Interventions: For families facing significant challenges, therapy can address underlying issues affecting the caregiving relationship, promoting healthier interactions and attachment patterns.

These interventions aim to support the child's emotional development and allow caregivers to reflect on their caregiving approaches, encouraging practices that nurture secure attachments.

Generational Patterns

Attachment styles do not exist in isolation but form part of a generational cycle. Parents often pass down attachment patterns to their children, and this transmission occurs as caregivers, consciously or unconsciously, replicate the caregiving styles they experienced in their childhoods. Understanding this cyclical nature is crucial for breaking anxious attachment patterns and fostering secure attachments in future generations.

Caregivers need to self-reflect and seek support if necessary to disrupt this cycle. Possibilities include:

- Exploring One's Attachment History: Caregivers can benefit from examining their attachment experiences and considering how these might influence their caregiving style.
- Seeking Therapeutic Support: Therapy can allow caregivers to process attachment-related experiences and develop healthier relational patterns.
- Educating Themselves on Secure Attachment Practices: Accessing resources on secure attachment can equip caregivers with strategies to build positive relationships with their children.

By addressing generational attachment patterns, caregivers can pave the way for more secure and emotionally fulfilling relationships for themselves and their children, breaking the cycle of anxious attachment and fostering a legacy of secure connections.

As we consider caregivers' multifaceted role in shaping attachment, it becomes clear that the journey toward secure or anxious attachment begins in the nuanced interplay of caregiving styles, emotional mirroring, and the interventions employed to nurture healthy attachments. Moreover, recognizing the generational transmission of attachment styles illuminates the pathway for fostering positive change, ensuring that future relationships are built on a foundation of security and mutual understanding.

Through mindful caregiving and support, we can influence the present attachment landscape and the relational terrain of future generations.

2.3 ATTACHMENT THROUGH THE AGES: HOW ANXIOUS ATTACHMENT EVOLVES OVER TIME

The landscape of our emotional world is ever-changing, molded by experiences, and shaped by time. Anxious attachment, with its roots entangled in the fabric of early interactions, does not stand still as we age. It shifts, morphs, and adapts as we journey through life's stages. This fluid evolution underscores the dynamic nature of attachment and its impact on our interactions and sense of self at various ages.

Developmental Transitions

From the playgrounds of childhood through the tumult of adolescence and into the complexities of adult life, anxious attachment reveals itself in various guises, influenced by the developmental challenges and social expectations of each stage.

- Childhood: In these formative years, children with anxious attachment might appear clingy, seeking constant validation from caregivers and peers. Their fear of separation or rejection can lead to heightened distress during transitions, such as starting school or facing social challenges.
- Adolescence: This phase amplifies the struggle for those with anxious attachment, as the drive for independence clashes with underlying insecurities. Teenagers might oscillate between a fierce desire for autonomy and an intense fear of losing connection, leading to turbulent relationships with family and peers.

- Adulthood: In adult relationships, anxious attachment often surfaces in the fear of abandonment and a pattern of seeking reassurance from partners. It can affect professional interactions, where criticism or conflict might be perceived as rejection, and in parenting, fears of repeating past cycles loom.

Each transition offers a mirror reflecting how anxious attachment colors our perceptions and dictates our responses to the world around us.

Trigger Events

Life's unpredictability ensures we face events that test our emotional resilience. For those with anxious attachment, specific experiences can intensify fears and trigger behaviors rooted in deep-seated insecurities.

- Relationship Milestones: Commitments, such as marriage or cohabitation, can provoke anxiety, stirring fears of eventual loss or rejection.
- Parenting: The arrival of children can resurrect unresolved attachment issues as new parents confront their fears and desires for their child's emotional well-being.
- Loss or Trauma: Experiences of loss, whether through separation, divorce, or bereavement, can act as a catalyst, exacerbating anxious attachment behaviors and fears of abandonment.
- Career Changes: Job loss or significant professional setbacks can trigger underlying insecurities, manifesting as fears of inadequacy and rejection.

While challenging, these events also present opportunities for reflection, growth, and healing, pushing individuals to confront and address their attachment-related fears.

Adaptive vs. Maladaptive

At their core, anxious attachment behaviors are survival strategies evolved to ensure closeness and care. However, the line between adaptive and maladaptive is thin, shaped by context and intensity.

- Adaptive: In some situations, the heightened sensitivity to others' emotional states and needs that characterize anxious attachment can foster deep empathy and care, strengthening social bonds and support networks.
- Maladaptive: More often, the pervasive fear of abandonment and the need for reassurance can strain relationships, leading to cycles of dependency and conflict. It can hinder personal growth, as the constant quest for external validation overshadows self-discovery and pursuing individual goals.

Recognizing when anxious attachment behaviors shift from being protective to restrictive is crucial in navigating the path toward healthier relational dynamics.

Resilience Factors

The journey from anxious attachment toward security is not predetermined but influenced by a constellation of factors that foster resilience and openness to change.

- Self-awareness: Recognizing and understanding one's attachment style illuminates the roots of fears and behaviors, paving the way for change.

- Supportive Relationships: Connections that offer consistency, empathy, and respect can serve as models for healthy interactions and secure attachment.
- Therapy and Counseling: Professional support provides a space to explore attachment issues, offering strategies for managing insecurities and building healthier relational patterns.
- Mindfulness and Self-compassion: Practices that encourage presence, acceptance, and kindness towards oneself can mitigate the impact of anxious attachment, reducing reactivity and fostering emotional balance.

These resilience factors do not erase the challenges of anxious attachment but offer tools and pathways for navigating its complexities, allowing for transformation and growth.

As we move through life, the expression and impact of anxious attachment evolve, influenced by developmental stages, life events, and our responses to them. Recognizing this attachment style's adaptive and maladaptive aspects is crucial in understanding its role in our lives. Moreover, acknowledging the factors contributing to resilience highlights the potential for change and growth, reminding us that our attachment style, while deeply rooted, is not immutable.

2.4 BREAKING THE CYCLE: UNDERSTANDING INTERGENERATIONAL TRANSMISSION

In human connections, the threads that weave the fabric of our attachment styles are often passed down through generations, subtly influencing how we interact with those closest to us. The intricate process of transmitting attachment patterns from generation to generation involves a complex interplay of behavior, emotion, and communication, not merely a matter of genetics. Recognizing and addressing this cycle is pivotal for those who wish to foster healthier relationships for themselves and future generations.

Mechanisms of Transmission

The transmission of attachment styles across generations operates through several mechanisms, each contributing to the continuity or alteration of attachment behaviors:

- Modeling and Mimicry: Children observe and internalize the attachment behaviors exhibited by their caregivers. This mimicry extends beyond childhood, shaping how they relate to others in adulthood.
- Emotional Communication: How emotions are expressed and managed within the family sets a template for children. Families that openly discuss and manage emotions healthily promote secure attachment, while environments discouraging emotional expression can sustain anxious attachment.
- Parenting Practices: The methods and approaches used in parenting, influenced by the caregiver's attachment style, directly impact the development of the child's attachment patterns. For example, a parent with an anxious attachment might overcompensate through overly protective behavior, inadvertently fostering dependency and anxiety in their child.

Awareness of these mechanisms empowers individuals to reflect on their behaviors and roots, opening pathways to intentional change.

Awareness and Change

Becoming conscious of the origins of one's attachment style is a vital step toward breaking the cycle of anxious attachment. This awareness allows individuals to:

- Reflect on Personal Attachment History: Acknowledging one's attachment experiences and their impact on current relationships is crucial. This reflection fosters understanding and empathy for oneself and one's caregivers, who also operate within the constraints of their attachment styles.
- Identify and Alter Maladaptive Patterns: Recognition of maladaptive attachment behaviors enables individuals to actively seek alternative responses. For instance, recognizing a tendency to seek excessive reassurance in relationships can prompt one to develop more self-reliant coping strategies.
- Choose Different Parenting Approaches: Awareness of their attachment style encourages parents to adopt parenting practices that nurture secure attachment, consciously choosing behaviors that differ from those they experienced.

This journey of awareness is not solitary but supported through resources, therapy, and community, reinforcing the commitment to change.

Therapeutic Approaches

Several therapeutic approaches have shown effectiveness in healing attachment wounds and guiding individuals and families toward healthier attachment patterns:

- Attachment-Based Family Therapy (ABFT): ABFT works to repair ruptures in the parent-child relationship, fostering emotional connectedness and secure attachment. By addressing unresolved attachment issues, this therapy helps the family develop healthier, more supportive relationships.
- Cognitive-behavioral therapy (CBT): Cognitive-behavioral therapy can help individuals recognize and change thoughts and behaviors stemming from anxious attachment, encouraging more secure relational patterns.
- Mindfulness-Based Interventions: Practices that encourage presence, acceptance, and self-compassion can help mitigate the anxiety and fear characteristic of insecure attachment, paving the way for more balanced emotional responses.

Engaging in these therapeutic practices offers a roadmap for individuals and families to navigate the complexities of attachment, heal past wounds, and build a foundation for secure relationships.

Community and Support Systems

Community and support systems play a crucial role in breaking the cycle of anxious attachment. These networks provide models of secure attachment, emotional support, and resources for learning and growth:

- Support Groups: Groups for parents, families, or individuals dealing with attachment issues offer a space for sharing experiences, challenges, and strategies for change. The collective wisdom and empathy found in these groups can be a powerful antidote to the isolation often felt by those with anxious attachment.

- Educational Workshops and Seminars: Community-based workshops on attachment, parenting, and emotional communication provide valuable knowledge and tools for fostering secure attachment. These educational opportunities encourage proactive steps towards healthier relationships.
- Mentorship and Role Models: Connecting with individuals who embody secure attachment can offer inspiration and guidance. Mentors, whether in formal or informal capacities, can demonstrate healthy relational dynamics and provide support in navigating relationship challenges.

The fabric of the community weaves a support network that holds individuals as they work to understand and transform their attachment styles. By engaging with these support systems, individuals receive the encouragement and resources needed for change and contribute to a culture of understanding and healing, extending the benefits of their growth beyond themselves to the broader community.

Recognizing the intergenerational transmission of attachment styles is critical in the journey toward healthier attachment patterns. Mechanisms of modeling, emotional communication, and parenting practices perpetuate these patterns, yet awareness, therapeutic intervention, and community support can break the cycle. This process, rooted in understanding and intention, opens up new possibilities for emotional health and fulfilling relationships, marking a departure from the past and a hopeful direction for the future.

2.5 THE IMPACT OF CULTURE ON ATTACHMENT STYLES

Diverse cultures richly weave the tapestry of human society, each imparting its unique colors and patterns onto the fabric of attachment. These cultural norms and values, often passed down through generations, profoundly influence how we form and perceive emotional bonds. Recognizing the profound effect of cultural background on attachment behaviors and perceptions of security invites a more nuanced understanding of our emotional landscapes and those of others around us.

Cultural Variations

Cultures around the globe present a kaleidoscope of practices and beliefs that shape the development of attachment styles. In some societies, emphasis on independence and self-reliance informs caregiving practices that may promote avoidant attachment traits, valuing autonomy over emotional expressiveness. Conversely, cultures prioritizing community and interconnectedness foster more secure or anxious attachments, emphasizing family bonds and collective well-being. These cultural influences guide the formation of attachment styles and shape the societal perceptions of what constitutes a 'secure base.'

- In societies valuing independence, children might be encouraged early to sleep alone, fostering self-soothing.
- Cultures emphasize familial closeness with multigenerational households, with children experiencing a wide circle of care.

Cross-Cultural Research

Recent studies illuminate the fascinating interplay between culture and attachment, revealing universal patterns and culturally specific nuances. Despite the diversity of upbringing practices across the globe, the need for a secure attachment base is a common thread, underscoring the universality of this human condition. However, the manifestation of secure or insecure attachment can significantly vary. For instance, research comparing Western and Eastern societies finds differences in the expression of attachment behaviors attributed to the cultural contexts that shape socialization practices and relational expectations.

- Studies show that while the proportion of secure attachment may be consistent, the expression of insecurity varies, with anxious attachment more prevalent in societies that emphasize communal values.

Cultural Competence

In addressing attachment issues, it becomes imperative to approach individuals and families with cultural competence, acknowledging and respecting the diverse family structures, practices, and values that inform attachment behaviors. Culturally competent care involves:

- Considering the cultural context of the individual's upbringing and current environment.
- Respecting cultural practices in caregiving and family dynamics.
- Adapting therapeutic interventions to align with cultural values and beliefs.

This approach ensures more effective support and intervention and fosters trust and understanding, which are crucial components in therapeutic relationships and support systems.

Global Perspectives

Adopting a global perspective on attachment enriches our understanding and appreciation of how humans connect and bond. It reminds us that while the need for secure attachments is a shared human experience, the paths to achieving these bonds are as diverse as the cultures that shape us. This global view encourages openness, curiosity, and respect for the myriad ways of nurturing connections, offering valuable insights for personal growth and the broader field of attachment research.

- Recognizing the universal need for connection alongside the diversity in its expression broadens our approach to supporting secure attachments.

In exploring the impact of culture on attachment styles, we uncover the layers of influence that our societal norms and values exert on our most intimate bonds. From the variations in caregiving practices across cultures to the insights gained from cross-cultural research, we see the intricate dance between individual development and cultural context. This exploration calls for cultural competence in addressing attachment issues, advocating for an approach that honors diversity while recognizing our shared needs for connection and security.

As we close this chapter, we can reflect on the intricate web of factors that shape our attachment styles, from the personal narratives of our childhood to the broad strokes of cultural influence. This understanding deepens our insight into the roots of our emotional behaviors and opens doors to embracing the richness of human diversity in forming connections. With this foundation, we look ahead to unraveling the complexities of anxious attachment as it plays out in the theater of adult relationships, continuing our quest for understanding, healing, and growth.

CHAPTER 3

Seeing love through anxious eyes

I magine sipping coffee across from someone dear to you, their words floating in the air, but your mind is miles away, tangled in a web of what-ifs and reading between lines that might not even exist. This imagined scene is often viewed through anxious eyes, where love is not just an emotion but a puzzle to be solved, a constant quest for reassurance in a sea of perceived instability. In this chapter, we'll peel back the layers of how anxious attachment colors our view of relationships and explore strategies for clearer, healthier perspectives.

Distorted Lenses

Anxious attachment can resemble a pair of glasses with a distorted lens, skewing our view of our partner's actions and intentions. A text replied to late or an offhand comment can spiral into a storm of worry and doubt. It's like watching a movie where the suspense music never stops, turning even benign scenes into moments of tension. This distortion can lead to misunderstandings, where one partner reacts not to what is happening but to what they fear might happen—for instance, interpreting a partner's need for some alone time not as a personal need for space but as a sign of waning affection.

Hyper-vigilance

Hyper-vigilance fuels this skewed perception, as individuals remain constantly alert for signs of rejection or disinterest from a partner. It's akin to having an emotional radar always on, scanning for threats, making it hard to relax into the relationship. This vigilance can be exhausting for the one experiencing it and their partner, who might feel under constant scrutiny. A helpful strategy here is mindfulness, which helps anchor thoughts in the present and calms the relentless scanning for signs of trouble. Scheduled check-ins with a partner can also help ease this vigilance by providing regular, set times for reassurance, reducing the need for constant monitoring.

Self-Worth and Reassurance

Underneath this need for constant reassurance lies a shaky foundation of self-worth. Anxious attachment often carries an underlying belief of not being good enough, making external validation from a partner crucial for self-esteem. It's like using a partner's affection as a mirror to reflect a sense of worth. Building self-worth outside the relationship is imperative—pursuing personal interests, setting individual goals, and fostering friendships can all contribute to a more stable sense of self that isn't solely dependent on a partner's validation.

Positive Feedback Loop

Recognizing and understanding these perceptions can initiate a positive feedback loop, where greater awareness leads to healthier relationship dynamics. Recognizing that anxious attachment can distort one's perceptions enables taking a step back, pausing to take a deep breath, and adopting a more objective perspective.

Open communication plays a crucial role here, where expressing feelings and fears can lead to reassurance and understanding from a partner. Thus, the relationship strengthens, providing tangible evidence against anxious thoughts and creating a cycle of positive interactions.

For those navigating the waters of anxious attachment, remember: you can clean the lens through which you view your relationship, tune the radar to be less sensitive, and firmly hold the mirror of self-worth in your own hands. By addressing these aspects of anxious attachment, individuals and couples can work towards a relationship characterized not by fear and doubt but by trust, understanding, and genuine connection.

3.2 THE SELF-FULFILLING PROPHECY OF ANXIOUS ATTACHMENT

Anxious attachment can often lead to a cycle where fears and behaviors inadvertently reinforce each other, acting out a self-fulfilling prophecy. At the heart of this cycle lies the expectation of rejection, a pervasive concern that drives actions that can, para-doxically, distance a partner.

- Expectation of Rejection: This anticipation stems from deeply ingrained beliefs about unworthiness and the fear that rejection is inevitable once a partner truly knows them. It's as if one is constantly waiting for the other shoe to drop, bracing for the pain of being left behind. This expectation can color interpretations of a partner's actions, leading to misread signals and heightened anxiety over the relationship's stability.
- Behavioral Patterns: The behaviors that emerge from this expectation can vary widely but often share a common

goal: to prevent the anticipated rejection from happening. Some might find themselves:

- Clinging tightly to their partner, fearing that any moment spent apart is an opportunity for the partner to realize their supposed flaws.
- Engaging in excessive communication, such as constant texting or calling, seeking reassurance that the relationship is secure.
- Asking for repeated affirmations of commitment stems from a place of vulnerability and can strain the relationship or push a partner away.

Though motivated by a desire to secure the bond, these actions can unfortunately lead to the outcome feared most. Feeling overwhelmed or controlled, the partner might withdraw, thus confirming the anxious individual's worst fears about their worthiness of love and connection.

- Breaking the Cycle: Interrupting this self-fulfilling prophecy requires a multifaceted approach, focusing on internal beliefs as much as external behaviors.

- Start by recognizing these patterns and questioning the evidence behind the fears driving them.
- Practice self-soothing techniques that can help manage anxiety in the moment, reducing the impulse to seek immediate reassurance from a partner.
- Cultivate a strong support network outside the romantic relationship, diversifying sources of emotional validation and reducing the pressure on the partnership.

- Set small, achievable goals for independence within the relationship, gradually building confidence in one's ability to be alone without being lonely.

- Role of Therapy: Engaging in individual or couples therapy can be instrumental in addressing and changing patterns of anxious attachment. A therapist can help individuals:

  - Explore the origins of their fears and expectations, often tracing back to early childhood experiences.
  - Develop healthier communication and relationship skills, focusing on expressing needs and desires that invite connection rather than demand reassurance.
  - Work on building self-esteem independent of the relationship, addressing the core beliefs about unworthiness that fuel the cycle of anxiety and clinginess.

Therapy can also offer couples a neutral space to navigate these dynamics, fostering understanding and empathy on both sides of the attachment equation. Through guided conversations, partners can learn how to support each other in breaking the cycle, creating a relationship dynamic that encourages security and mutual growth.

Addressing the self-fulfilling prophecy of anxious attachment requires understanding the underlying fears, recognizing the behaviors they provoke, and actively working towards healthier patterns of interaction. Through introspection, support, and professional guidance, it's possible to rewrite the script, fostering relationships based on trust, mutual respect, and genuine connection rather than fear and insecurity.

3.3 NAVIGATING RELATIONSHIP DYNAMICS WITH ANXIOUS ATTACHMENT

In the panorama of relationships, each interaction and shared silence hold layers of unspoken words and emotions. For those experiencing anxious attachment, these layers feel more like a labyrinth, where every turn could lead to reassurance or a deepening sense of insecurity. Navigating this labyrinth requires self-awareness and a shared language of understanding and support within the relationship.

Understanding Triggers

Triggers in the context of anxious attachment are like invisible threads that, when pulled, unravel a tapestry of fears and insecurities. These can range from a partner's offhand comment to routine or social media activity changes. Recognizing these triggers is the first step toward disarming them. It involves:

- Reflecting on Past Experiences: Often, triggers are rooted in past relationships or early childhood experiences. Identifying these roots helps in understanding why specific actions or words stir anxiety.
- Observation and Journaling: Keeping a journal of moments when anxiety spikes in the relationship can reveal patterns, helping to pinpoint specific triggers.
- Self-Questioning: When feeling triggered, asking oneself, "What am I afraid of in this moment?" can help distinguish between present reality and past fears.

This understanding paves the way for more effective communication and coping strategies, reducing the power triggers have over the relationship dynamics.

Communication Strategies

Effective communication acts as a bridge over troubled waters in relationships marked by anxious attachment. It's about expressing needs and concerns in ways that invite understanding rather than conflict. Key strategies include:

- Use of 'I' Statements: Framing concerns as personal feelings rather than accusations ("I feel anxious when we don't talk about our plans" vs. "You never tell me what's happening") helps in reducing defensiveness.
- Expressing Needs Clearly: Being upfront about what you need for reassurance, whether regular check-ins or verbal affirmations, clarifies expectations.
- Active Listening: This involves fully engaging with what your partner is saying, free from the urge to formulate a response while they are still talking. It ensures that both partners feel heard and valued.
- Scheduled Discussions: Setting aside regular time to discuss the relationship allows both partners to prepare emotionally, reducing the likelihood of reactive responses.

These strategies cultivate a culture of openness and mutual respect, where individuals can share feelings and needs without fearing judgment or escalation.

Building Trust

Trust is the bedrock of any healthy relationship, yet for someone with anxious attachment, trust can feel like a fortress constantly under siege. Building trust is a gradual process, requiring patience and consistent effort from both partners. Some approaches include:

- Transparency: Openly sharing thoughts, feelings, and intentions builds a foundation of honesty and reliability.
- Reliability: Following through on promises and commitments, no matter how small, reinforces trust.
- Understanding and Patience: Recognizing that building trust is a journey, not a destination, allows for the ebbs and flows of progress.
- Therapeutic Support: Sometimes, external help from a therapist can guide partners in establishing or re-establishing trust, providing tools and techniques tailored to their needs.

These actions weave a stronger, more resilient bond incrementally, where trust can flourish despite the fears and insecurities accompanying anxious attachment.

Partner Support

The role of a supportive partner in navigating the challenges of anxious attachment is essential. It's about co-navigating the labyrinth, guiding the path ahead. Ways in which partners can offer support include:

- Educating Themselves: Understanding anxious attachment allows a partner to empathize with the fears and behaviors it can provoke.
- Reassuring Proactively: Sometimes, offering reassurance before anxiety escalates can prevent a spiral of worry.
- Setting Healthy Boundaries: Clear boundaries ensure that support does not become an enabling dependency.
- Encouraging Professional Help: Supporting a partner in seeking therapy or counseling can be invaluable in addressing anxious attachment more deeply.

A supportive stance fosters a relationship environment where addressing anxious attachment with compassion and empathy is prioritized over fear or frustration.

Navigating relationship dynamics with anxious attachment is about more than managing fears; it's about building a shared language of love and support that transcends these insecurities. This process requires patience, understanding, and a commitment to growth from both partners. Through this collaborative effort, relationships can become a source of strength and stability, even in the face of anxiety and fear.

3.4 THE JEALOUS MIND: UNDERSTANDING AND OVERCOMING JEALOUSY

Jealousy, a complex emotion often entangled with anxious attachment, weaves a challenging relationship pattern. It stems from a place deep within where fears of not being enough or losing someone dear cast long shadows over love and connection. This section aims to shed light on the multifaceted nature of jealousy, differentiating it from envy and offering strategies for navigating these turbulent waters with grace and understanding.

Roots of Jealousy

In anxious attachment, fears deeply rooted in past experiences of inadequacy and abandonment sow the seeds of jealousy. This emotional response is not so much about the actions of another but rather about what those actions signify to someone grappling with anxious attachment. The fear that a partner's attention or affection might wane, redirected towards someone else, triggers intense jealousy. This emotional turmoil often springs from unresolved issues of self-worth and a pervasive anxiety about being left alone.

Jealousy vs. Envy

While jealousy and envy are often used interchangeably in everyday language, they describe distinct emotional experiences, especially when viewed through anxious attachment.

- Jealousy arises when we fear a third party could threaten a valuable relationship. It's a relational triangle in which the perceived threat to the bond sparks jealousy.
- Conversely, envy occurs when we desire attributes, possessions, or qualities that someone else has. It's a two-way dynamic, focusing on what we lack compared to others.

Understanding this distinction is crucial. While envy might cause discomfort or dissatisfaction with one's situation, jealousy, especially in intimate relationships, can lead to conflict, mistrust, and, in some cases, the erosion of the connection one fears losing.

Managing Jealous Thoughts

Navigating through the stormy seas of jealous thoughts requires a deliberate and mindful approach. Here are strategies to help calm these turbulent waters:

- Identify the Trigger: Recognize what specific situations or behaviors ignite feelings of jealousy. Is it when your partner mentions a particular person or when they spend time away from you? Pinpointing triggers can help address the root cause of jealousy.
- Reframe the Narrative: Challenge the automatic thoughts that fuel jealousy. Remember that these thoughts are not facts but interpretations colored by anxious attachment.

Ask yourself, "Is there evidence to support my fears, or am I jumping to conclusions based on my insecurities?"

- Self-compassion Practice: Practice self-compassion to comfort feelings of inadequacy, which lie at the core of jealousy. Remind yourself of your worth and value in the relationship, independent of external validations.
- Mindfulness and Grounding Techniques: When jealousy feels overwhelming, grounding techniques such as focused breathing or mindfulness meditation can help bring you back to the present moment, reducing the intensity of the emotion.

Open Dialogue

Maintaining an open and honest dialogue with your partner is the key to navigating jealousy in a relationship. Open communication doesn't mean voicing every jealous thought but instead constructively discussing feelings of insecurity. Here's how to approach these conversations:

- Choose the Right Moment: Find a calm, neutral time to talk when neither of you is stressed or defensive.
- Express Your Feelings Without Blame: Use "I" statements to express your feelings without blaming your partner. For example, "I feel insecure when you spend so much time talking with your ex. I know it's my issue, but I could use reassurance."
- Listen Actively: Allow your partner to share their perspective without interruption. Understanding their view can help alleviate fears and build trust.
- Collaborate on Solutions: Work together to find ways to address the feelings of jealousy. Solutions involve setting boundaries that both are comfortable with and finding

ways your partner can help reassure you without feeling controlled.

By approaching jealousy with honesty, compassion, and a willingness to understand each other's perspectives, couples can strengthen their bond, turning a potential wedge into a building block for deeper intimacy and trust. Facing jealousy head-on, acknowledging its roots in anxious attachment, and working through it with open communication and self-reflection pave the way for relationships that are not just surviving but thriving, free from the shadows of doubt and fear.

3.5 COMMUNICATING NEEDS WITHOUT FEAR

When navigating the waters of a relationship with an anxious attachment style, expressing needs and desires can often feel like navigating through a thick fog—daunting and unclear. Yet, understanding and communicating these needs is akin to sending out a beacon of light, guiding your relationship towards a shore of mutual understanding and deeper connection. Let's explore how we can transform vulnerability into a shared strength.

Identifying Needs

Before communicating our needs, we must clearly understand what they are. This clarity often eludes us, as our actual needs might be buried under layers of fears and insecurities. To unearth these needs:

- Reflect on moments of discontent or frustration in your relationship. Ask yourself what was missing or desired in those instances.
- Consider your values and what aspects of a relationship

are non-negotiable for you. Is it consistency, transparency, affection, or something else?
- Pay attention to physical and emotional responses in different situations. These reactions can be indicators of more profound needs.

By doing this reflective work, we can distinguish between superficial wants and core emotional needs, setting the stage for open and honest communication.

Assertive Communication

Assertiveness is the bridge between recognizing your needs and having them met within the relationship. It involves expressing yourself clearly and respectfully without encroaching on your partner's boundaries. For those of us with anxious attachment, practicing assertiveness allows us to step away from passive or aggressive communication patterns, fostering a healthier dynamic. Tips for practicing assertive communication include:

- Use clear, direct language that focuses on specific behaviors rather than generalizations.
- Maintain open body language and eye contact to convey sincerity and confidence.
- Be prepared for various responses and remain open to discussion and compromise.

Assertiveness is not about demanding compliance but about inviting dialogue. Like any other skill, it improves with practice.

Vulnerability and Strength

In the heart of assertive communication lies vulnerability, the willingness to show our true selves, needs, and desires. Far from being a weakness, vulnerability is a testament to strength, a courageous act that fosters intimacy and trust in a relationship. When we express our needs transparently, we offer our partners the opportunity to understand us truly and, in turn, to be understood. This mutual vulnerability becomes the bedrock of a robust and resilient relationship. Embracing vulnerability means:

- Recognizing the strength in asking for what you need and acknowledging that it's okay not to have all the answers.
- Understanding that vulnerability is reciprocal – as you open up, you create a space for your partner to do the same.
- Seeing each act of vulnerability as a step towards building a deeper, more authentic connection.

Feedback and Reassurance

Once we've communicated our needs, seeking feedback and reassurance is natural. However, the key is to seek this in constructive and healthy ways rather than from a place of insecurity. We can achieve this by:

- Setting aside time for regular check-ins with your partner, where both of you can share feelings, needs, and feedback in a calm, supportive environment.
- Asking for specific reassurance that feels meaningful to you while being open to how your partner can provide it.
- Recognizing and appreciating your partner's effort to meet your needs, even if it's not exactly as you envisioned.

In seeking feedback and reassurance, we aim to create a dialogue that strengthens the relationship, ensuring both partners feel valued and heard.

As we wrap up this exploration of communicating needs without fear, we find that the essence lies in understanding ourselves, asserting our needs confidently, embracing vulnerability as a form of strength, and engaging in constructive feedback. This approach enriches our relationships and aligns with our journey toward emotional freedom and deeper connections. With these insights, we are better equipped to navigate the complexities of attachment and relationships, moving forward with a clearer vision and a stronger voice.

As we transition into the next chapter, we understand that communication is not just about being heard but also about listening, adapting, and growing together.

the path towards inner harmony

In the quiet moments before the dawn, when the world is still, our minds often speak the loudest, replaying the day's events, echoing our fears, and sometimes turning against us with a chorus of self-criticism. This inner dialogue, especially for those grappling with anxious attachment, can feel like a relentless critic, always ready to highlight flaws and fan the flames of insecurity. Yet, within this challenge lies an opportunity for profound transformation. It's about turning down the volume of negative self-talk and tuning into a narrative of kindness and self-compassion. Here, we'll explore strategies to rewrite the script of your inner dialogue, fostering a more supportive and empowering conversation with yourself.

Self-criticism and Anxious Attachment

The link between anxious attachment and self-criticism is akin to a well-worn path in a dense forest—the more it's traveled, the more defined it becomes. For someone with anxious attachment, this path is often cluttered with doubts about their worthiness of love and fear of abandonment. These fears can fuel a critical inner voice that questions one's value and amplifies insecurities.

- Real-life example: After a disagreement with a friend, someone with anxious attachment might replay the conversation, blaming themselves for the conflict and questioning their worthiness as a friend.

Breaking free from this cycle involves recognizing these patterns and understanding that this critical voice, though trying to protect you from hurt, often does more harm than good.

Challenging Negative Thoughts

Challenging and reframing negative thoughts is like learning a new language—the language of self-kindness. This process involves several steps:

1. Catch and Identify: Notice when you're being self-critical. Identify the specific thoughts and write them down.
2. Question and Challenge: Ask yourself, "Is this thought true? Is it helpful?" Consider what you would say to a friend in the same situation.
3. Reframe: Rewrite the thought from a more compassionate and realistic perspective.

- Exercise: Create a two-column chart. In the left column, jot down a recent self-critical thought. On the right, write a kinder, more objective response.

This practice doesn't erase negative thoughts but changes how you relate to them, reducing their impact over time.

Mindfulness and Self-Compassion

Mindfulness and self-compassion are twin beacons of light in the journey towards silencing the inner critic. Mindfulness encourages presence and acceptance, helping to observe thoughts without judgment. Self-compassion adds a layer of kindness, treating yourself with the same care and understanding you would offer a dear friend.

- Mindfulness practice: Spend a few minutes each day sitting quietly, focusing on your breath. When thoughts arise, acknowledge them without judgment and gently bring your focus back to your breath.
- Self-compassion break: Whenever you catch yourself in a spiral of self-criticism, place a hand over your heart. Remind yourself, "This is a moment of suffering. Suffering is a part of life. May I be kind to myself in this moment."

These practices anchor you in the present, creating space between you and your thoughts and fostering a more compassionate relationship with yourself.

Seeking Professional Help

Sometimes, the inner critic can feel too powerful to tackle alone. Seeking professional help from a therapist or counselor familiar with anxious attachment can provide the support and guidance needed to navigate this challenging terrain. Therapy offers a safe space to explore the origins of your self-critical thoughts, understand their connection to your attachment style, and develop strategies to cultivate a more supportive inner dialogue.

- When to seek help: If negative self-talk impacts your daily life, relationships, or well-being, it might be time to seek professional support.
- What to expect: Therapy can involve exploring your history, identifying triggers for self-criticism, and learning new coping strategies. It's a collaborative process tailored to your unique needs and goals.

Therapy is not a sign of weakness but a courageous step towards healing and growth, offering tools and insights that can empower you to rewrite the narrative of your inner dialogue.

In navigating the path towards inner harmony, the goal is not to silence the inner critic entirely—that voice may always be a part of you. Instead, it's about changing the conversation and learning to meet yourself with understanding, kindness, and compassion. You can foster a more positive and empowering inner dialogue by challenging negative thoughts, embracing mindfulness and self-compassion, and seeking support when needed. This shift enhances your relationship with yourself and enriches your connections with others, creating ripples of positivity that extend far beyond the confines of anxious attachment.

4.2 STRESS AND ANXIETY: THE PHYSICAL COST OF ANXIOUS ATTACHMENT

Body-Mind Connection

Reflect for a moment on how your body reacts when stress or anxiety takes hold. Perhaps your heart races, your breath quickens, or a knot forms in your stomach. These are not just fleeting sensations but signals of the deep connection between our emotional state and physical well-being. Anxious attachment, with its roots entangled in fear and insecurity, can lead to a constant state of stress, putting the body on high alert. This prolonged state of vigilance can have tangible physical repercussions, from disrupted sleep patterns to heightened blood pressure, illustrating the intricate dance between the mind and the body. Understanding this connection is the first step toward addressing the physical toll of anxious attachment.

- Physical manifestations can include insomnia, muscle tension, digestive issues, and fatigue, all of which compound the emotional strain of anxious attachment.
- Chronic stress linked to anxious attachment might also weaken the immune system, making one more susceptible to illnesses and prolonging recovery times.

Acknowledging these impacts encourages a proactive approach to managing stress and fostering well-being that encompasses mind and body.

Stress Management Techniques

Recognizing stress's multifaceted impact, integrating stress management techniques into daily life emerges as a crucial strategy. These techniques offer relief and serve as preventive measures, buffering the body against the potential physical strain of anxious attachment.

- Deep Breathing Exercises: Simple yet powerful, deep breathing can calm the nervous system, reducing immediate stress levels. Try inhaling deeply for a count of four, holding for a count of four, and exhaling slowly for a count of eight.
- Regular Physical Activity: Exercise releases endorphins, natural mood elevators that can counteract stress. Activities like walking, yoga, or dancing can be especially

beneficial, offering both physical release and mental relaxation.

- Progressive Muscle Relaxation: This technique involves tensing and relaxing different muscle groups in the body, promoting physical and mental calm. Starting from the toes and moving upward can help identify and release tension held in the body.
- Structured Relaxation Time: Dedicate a portion of your day to relaxation, engaging in activities that bring you joy and calm. Whether reading, gardening, or listening to music, this time can be a daily reset for stress levels.

Incorporating these techniques into your routine can help manage the stress and anxiety that often accompany anxious attachment, offering a pathway to greater physical and emotional balance.

Holistic Well-being

Adopting a holistic perspective on well-being recognizes that true health encompasses physical fitness, mental clarity, and emotional stability. This approach is particularly relevant for individuals with anxious attachment, for whom emotional distress can manifest in physical symptoms. A holistic strategy might include:

- Nutritional Awareness: Pay attention to nutrition and choose foods that support mood and energy levels. Omega-3 fatty acids, found in fish and nuts, and magnesium-rich foods like leafy greens can be especially beneficial for stress management.
- Adequate Sleep: Prioritizing sleep, recognizing its role in emotional regulation and physical health. Establishing a calming bedtime routine can improve sleep quality, enhancing overall resilience to stress.

- Mind-Body Practices: Engaging in practices that connect the mind and body, such as tai chi, qigong, or meditation, can improve stress management and foster a sense of inner peace.
- Social Connections: Nurturing supportive relationships improves emotional well-being and offers a buffer against stress. Spending time with loved ones or engaging in community activities can provide emotional support and a sense of belonging.

Embracing this holistic view encourages a multifaceted approach to well-being, where care for the body and mind goes hand in hand.

Creating a Self-Care Plan

A personalized self-care plan acts as a roadmap for navigating the challenges of living with anxious attachment, offering a structured approach to managing stress and fostering well-being. Developing this plan involves:

- Identifying Stressors: Pinpoint the specific aspects of anxious attachment that trigger stress for you, whether it's fear of abandonment, need for reassurance, or difficulty trusting partners.
- Choosing Techniques: Based on the stressors identified, select stress management techniques that resonate with you. Incorporate a mix of immediate relief methods, like deep breathing, and long-term strategies, such as regular exercise.
- Setting Goals: Establish clear, achievable goals for your self-care practices. Start small, with five minutes of meditation daily or a weekly yoga class, and gradually build from there.

- Monitoring Progress: Keep a journal to track your self-care activities, noting how they impact your stress levels and overall well-being. This record can help fine-tune your approach and ensure it meets your evolving needs.

A self-care plan tailored to the nuances of anxious attachment can serve as a powerful tool in your well-being arsenal, offering structured support as you navigate the complexities of stress and anxiety. With each step taken towards self-care, you reinforce the commitment to your well-being, laying the foundation for a healthier, more balanced life.

4.3 THE PARADOX OF SOLITUDE: ALONE BUT NOT LONELY

The quiet of being alone offers a canvas much broader than the confines of loneliness. In these stretches of solitude, we find undisturbed soil for growth and self-exploration. Far from the shadow of loneliness, solitude is a beacon, illuminating paths to internal peace and fostering a profound understanding of self that underpins secure relationships.

Embracing Solitude

The art of embracing solitude lies in recognizing its value as a sanctuary for introspection and rejuvenation. In moments by oneself, the mind finds freedom from the constant hum of external expectations and social dynamics. Within the embrace of solitude lies the opportunity to engage deeply with personal thoughts, feelings, and aspirations. This engagement is not a retreat from the world but a means to connect more authentically with oneself and others.

- Mindful Practices: Integrating mindful practices into periods of solitude can enhance the quality of this time. Activities like meditation or simply sitting in nature without the distraction of devices allow for a deeper connection with the present moment and oneself.

Differentiating Solitude from Loneliness

Understanding the distinction between solitude and loneliness is crucial. Solitude is a chosen state of being alone, often fulfilling and enriching. Loneliness, in contrast, is a feeling of sadness or discomfort about being alone, marked by a sense of disconnect from others.

- Reflection Exercise: Consider times when you have felt both solitude and loneliness. Reflect on the emotions, thoughts, and physical sensations associated with each. This exercise can help you recognize the differences and choose solitude over loneliness.

Finding Comfort in One's Own Company

Discovering joy and comfort in one's own company transforms solitude from a condition to be avoided into a cherished space. Cultivating a relationship with oneself that is as compassionate and understanding as those we strive for with others lays the groundwork for this transformation.

- Self-Date Ideas: Schedule regular 'self-dates' – dedicated times to do activities that you enjoy alone, whether it's visiting a museum, taking a long walk, or having a meal at a favorite restaurant. These moments reinforce the pleasure of your own company.

Personal Development

When embraced, solitude becomes a powerful ally in personal development. It allows for an uninterrupted focus on individual goals, interests, and areas of growth. This dedicated time for self-improvement and reflection can lead to discoveries about personal values, strengths, and areas where change is desired.

- Skill Building: Use time alone to learn new skills or explore hobbies. Whether learning a language, playing an instrument, or crafting, these activities enrich personal skills and enhance self-esteem and a sense of accomplishment.
- Journaling: Keeping a journal offers a space for self-expression and reflection. Writing about experiences, emotions, and aspirations helps clarify thoughts and set meaningful goals.

In solitude, there is an unspoken promise of growth, a quiet understanding that being alone does not mean being less. It is an opportunity to build a foundation of self-awareness and self-compassion that supports healthier, more secure attachments in relationships. By embracing solitude, differentiating it from loneliness, finding joy in one's own company, and focusing on personal development, solitude becomes a momentary and vital part of a balanced, fulfilling life.

4.4 BUILDING SELF-ESTEEM FROM THE GROUND UP

Self-esteem is the lens through which we view our worthiness and capabilities. The inner voice whispers encouragement or doubts as we face life's challenges. For those navigating the waters of anxious attachment, this voice often leans towards criticism, eroding confidence and reinforcing fears of unworthiness. However, we can nurture and enrich the soil from which self-esteem grows, allowing us to cultivate a more positive self-view.

Foundations of Self-Esteem

Self-esteem is nurtured from our earliest interactions, reflecting how valued and capable we feel. Anxious attachment, characterized by fears of abandonment and a hunger for external validation, can shake this foundation. It creates a dependency on others for our self-worth, leaving us vulnerable to the ebbs and flows of relationships. Understanding this, we see the need to fortify our self-esteem from within, grounding it in our perceptions of self rather than the unpredictable affirmations from others. This shift involves recognizing our intrinsic value, independent of external validation.

Activities to Boost Self-Esteem

Activities that strengthen self-esteem share a common thread: they affirm our competence and worth through tangible achievements and self-acknowledgment. Consider incorporating these practices into your routine:

- Goal Setting: Identify small, achievable goals that align with your interests and values. Successfully reaching these targets reinforces your sense of capability and accomplishment.
- Skill Development: Dedicate time to learning new skills or honing existing ones. Mastery in areas of interest boosts self-confidence and provides a fulfilling outlet for self-expression.
- Self-appreciation Logs: Keep a daily or weekly log of actions or qualities you are proud of. This practice

encourages focusing on your strengths and achievements, countering the tendency to overlook them.

These activities are bricks in the construction of a more solid foundation of self-esteem, each success story adding to the sense of self-worth.

Role of Positive Affirmations

Positive affirmations are powerful tools in rewriting the narratives we hold about ourselves. They counter the often automatic negative thoughts dominating our inner dialogue, especially in moments of doubt or insecurity. Incorporating affirmations involves:

- Crafting Personal Affirmations: Develop affirmations that resonate with your desired self-view. These should be in the present tense, positive, and specific, such as "I am capable of handling whatever comes my way."
- Routine Integration: Integrate affirmations into your daily routine. You can integrate affirmation through morning recitations, Post-it notes in visible locations, or phone reminders.
- Emotional Engagement: As you practice affirmations, strive to feel the truth of the words, not just recite them. This emotional engagement is central to their effectiveness.

Through consistent practice, positive affirmations can shift the tide of internal dialogue, promoting a more supportive and encouraging self-view.

Support Systems

While the journey to bolstered self-esteem is deeply personal, it doesn't have to be solitary. Support systems are critical in reflecting and reinforcing our worth, especially when self-doubt looms. A robust support system might include:

- Trusted Friends and Family: Relationships that provide honest, positive feedback and encouragement can mirror our worth, reflecting the strengths we might overlook.
- Community Groups or Clubs: Engaging in groups that share your interests or values can offer a sense of belonging and validation, affirming your place and value within a community.
- Professional Support: Therapists or counselors can offer guidance and affirmation, helping to navigate the challenges of building self-esteem with understanding and expertise.

By building and relying on a support system, we ensure that even when our self-esteem falters, we don't face these challenges alone. These connections remind us of our worth, encourage our growth, and celebrate our successes alongside us.

In the garden of self-esteem, we are both the gardener and the soil, capable of nurturing growth through attention, care, and the right conditions. From understanding the fragile foundations on which self-esteem might rest for those with anxious attachment to engaging in activities that affirm our worth, crafting empowering affirmations, and leaning on supportive relationships, the tools for cultivating a stronger self-view are within reach. With each step taken on this path, the voice of self-encouragement grows louder, guiding us toward a place where our worth is recognized and cherished, deeply rooted in the understanding of our inherent value.

4.5 EMBRACING INDEPENDENCE: THE PATH TO EMOTIONAL FREEDOM

Achieving emotional independence is akin to cultivating a garden within oneself, a sanctuary of self-sufficiency where the fruits of personal growth can flourish. This task presents distinct challenges for those entwined in the vines of anxious attachment. Emotional independence signifies a state where one's emotional well-being doesn't solely hinge on the actions or affections of others. It's about fostering an inner resilience that allows for a healthy detachment and self-reliance, crucial for navigating the complexities of relationships without losing oneself in the process.

Navigating towards emotional independence involves several actionable steps. Begin by diversifying interests and investing time in hobbies or activities that resonate with you. These pursuits enrich your life and reinforce your sense of self, independent of your relationships. Equally important is setting personal goals and milestones that reflect your aspirations and values. Achieving these goals underscores your capabilities and strengths, reinforcing your confidence and sense of autonomy.

A cornerstone in the architecture of emotional independence is establishing and respecting personal boundaries. Boundaries act as the protective walls of your emotional garden, delineating where you end and others begin. They are essential for maintaining your integrity and preventing the erosion of your sense of self in the face of external pressures or demands. Setting boundaries involves clear communication of your needs and limits and the willingness to enforce them, even when faced with resistance. This practice fosters a balanced relationship dynamic where your needs are respected and met without compromising your autonomy.

Celebrating every stride towards independence is crucial. Acknowledge each step, no matter how small, as a testament to your progress. This acknowledgment serves as a reminder of your growth, reinforcing your journey toward emotional freedom. It shifts the focus from the destination to the journey itself, highlighting the value in each experience and lesson learned.

In weaving the narrative of this chapter, we've traversed the landscape of emotional independence, highlighting the significance of developing interests outside of relationships, setting achievable personal goals, the critical role of boundaries, and the importance of celebrating each step forward. This exploration contributes to a more fulfilling, autonomous life and lays the groundwork for more fulfilling and balanced relationships.

As we close this chapter, remember that the path to emotional independence is not a solitary journey but a series of steps taken in the company of one's own evolving self. It's about nurturing a relationship with oneself that is as compassionate and fulfilling as those we seek with others. Having sown the seeds of self-reliance, we look ahead to the next chapter, where we will explore the dynamics of fostering healthier relationships, understanding that our well-being does not solely depend on the presence or actions of others but blossoms from within.

CHAPTER 5

cultivating secure foundations

Picture a tree in full bloom, its branches heavy with fruit and leaves whispering in the wind. Its strength and beauty are undeniable, yet none of this would be possible without the roots that anchor it firmly to the ground, drawing up the nutrients and water it needs to thrive. In many ways, our emotional landscape resembles this tree, with secure attachment forming the roots that nourish and stabilize us, allowing us to grow and flourish in our relationships.

Understanding Secure Attachment

Secure attachment is like the fertile soil that feeds the tree, essential for healthy growth. Several vital elements characterize it:

- Emotional Availability: Just as a tree needs sunlight to thrive, our relationships need the warmth of emotional availability. Emotional availability means being there for each other, physically and emotionally, ready to share joys, sorrows, and everything in between.

- Responsiveness: Like the rain that quenches the tree's thirst, responsiveness in relationships refreshes and reassures us. It's about tuning in to our partner's needs and emotions and responding in a supportive way.
- Positive View of Self and Others: A tree's strength comes from its robust roots, just as our confidence in relationships stems from a positive view of ourselves and our partners. Believing in our worthiness of love and our partner's goodwill lays the groundwork for trust and intimacy.

Building Trust

Trust is the cornerstone of secure attachment, as vital as the nutrients the tree's roots draw up. Here are practical ways to cultivate trust:

- Keep promises, no matter how small they seem. If you say you'll call at a specific time, do it. This consistency builds reliability.
- Practice honesty, even when it's challenging. Openly sharing your feelings and vulnerabilities fosters a deeper connection.
- Show up for each other in moments of need and in everyday life; being present signals to your partner that they can count on you.

Consistency and Reliability

Just as a tree relies on the steady cycle of seasons, our relationships flourish with consistency and reliability. Life doesn't have to be devoid of surprises; instead, there's a dependable foundation to which to return. For instance, establishing routines, like a weekly date night or daily check-in calls, can create a rhythm of reliability that nurtures trust and security.

Self-Validation

In the quest for secure attachment, validating ourselves is as crucial as the rain to the tree. It's about affirming our worth, honoring our emotions, and reducing the dependence on external validation for our self-esteem and happiness. Here are some strategies:

- Reflect on Your Strengths: Regularly take the time to acknowledge what you love about yourself. Journaling or meditation are supportive practices for self-reflection.
- Set Personal Goals: Achieve milestones that matter to you, whether in your career, hobbies, or personal growth. Celebrating these achievements boosts your sense of self-efficacy.
- Practice Self-Compassion: Treat yourself with the same kindness and understanding you'd offer a friend. When you stumble or face setbacks, remind yourself that perfection is not the goal; growth is.

By nurturing these pillars of secure attachment, we lay the foundation for relationships that are not only enduring but also enriching, allowing us to stand tall and resilient, much like the tree in full bloom. With roots anchored in trust, emotional availability, and self-validation, we're better equipped to weather the storms and droughts that inevitably come our way, knowing that our foundation is resilient and our capacity for growth limitless.

5.2 REWRITING THE ATTACHMENT SCRIPT: COGNITIVE BEHAVIORAL TECHNIQUES

All too often, the narratives we tell ourselves about who we are and how we fit into relationships stem from deep-seated beliefs formed in our earliest years. These beliefs, especially when tinged with the hues of anxious attachment, can distort our view of ourselves and our capacity to create healthy, fulfilling relationships. Yet, with the right tools and determination, these scripts can be rewritten, paving the way for a more secure attachment style.

Identifying Negative Thought Patterns

The initial step involves shining a light on the negative thought patterns that cloud our relationship landscape. These thoughts, often automatic and deeply ingrained, can include beliefs such as "I'm not worthy of love" or "I will be rejected if I show my true self." To unearth these patterns, it can be helpful to:

- Maintain a thought diary over a few weeks, jotting down instances when you feel particularly anxious or insecure in your relationships. Note the thoughts that accompany these feelings.
- Look for patterns in these thoughts. Do common themes or fears arise?
- Consider the origins of these thoughts. Can you trace them back to specific experiences or relationships in your past?

This critical awareness allows us to challenge and transform these thoughts in the following steps.

Behavioral Experiments

Behavioral experiments form the bridge between recognizing negative thought patterns and actively challenging them. These experiments involve testing our beliefs in real-life scenarios, observing the outcomes, and reflecting on the dissonance between our expectations and reality. For instance:

- Suppose you believe expressing needs will drive others away; experiment by voicing a small need or preference in a safe relationship. Observe the response.
- If the fear of being alone feels overwhelming, spend an evening engaging in a self-soothing activity. Reflect on the experience and any emotions it evokes.

These experiments can provide concrete evidence that challenges our negative beliefs, showing us that our fears, while valid, may not always align with reality.

Reframing Experiences

Our past experiences, especially those that have been painful or traumatic, can cast long shadows over our present relationships. Reframing these experiences doesn't mean denying the pain they caused but instead shifting our perspective. Techniques for reframing include:

- Looking for lessons or strengths that emerged from challenging experiences. How have these experiences contributed to your growth or resilience?
- Practicing gratitude for the relationships and experiences that have been sources of joy and support, acknowledging their role in your life.

- Seeking alternative explanations for painful events reduces the tendency to blame oneself or view the event as a reflection of one's inherent unworthiness.

By reframing past experiences, we can see them as chapters in our story that, while significant, don't define the entirety of our narrative.

Creating a New Narrative

The culmination of identifying negative thought patterns, conducting behavioral experiments, and reframing experiences is the creation of a new narrative about oneself and one's capacity for healthy relationships. This narrative is built on self-compassion, resilience, and a more realistic assessment of our worth and capabilities. Steps to create this new narrative include:

- Write a letter to yourself from the perspective of a compassionate friend, highlighting your strengths, resilience, and capacity for growth and love.
- Visualize your ideal self in relationships—how you communicate, how you handle conflict, what makes you feel secure—and set small, achievable goals to move closer to this vision.
- Celebrate the small victories, whether successfully navigating a difficult conversation, spending a rewarding evening alone, or simply catching and challenging a negative thought.

This new narrative is not a fixed script but a living document that evolves with you as you grow and navigate the complexities of relationships. It serves as a reminder of your journey, growth, and inherent worth, guiding you toward more secure attachments and fulfilling connections.

In rewriting our attachment script through cognitive behavioral techniques, we engage in a process of transformation that reaches far beyond the confines of our relationships. It's a journey that nurtures self-understanding, challenges old fears, and opens the door to new possibilities for connection and growth. With each step, we move closer to a version of ourselves that approaches relationships with confidence, openness, and a deep-seated sense of security, ready to give and receive love in all its forms.

5.3 EMOTIONAL REGULATION: TECHNIQUES FOR MANAGING INTENSE FEELINGS

In the landscape of our emotional lives, the ability to navigate and regulate our feelings stands as a beacon, guiding us through tumultuous and serene moments. Emotional regulation is not about suppressing what we feel but learning to understand and manage our emotions, ensuring they don't overwhelm us or dictate our reactions in ways we might later regret. This skill is particularly vital for those of us who might find ourselves caught in the storm of anxious attachment, where emotions can sometimes feel like uncharted waters.

Recognizing Emotional Triggers

The first step in mastering emotional regulation involves shining a light on the triggers that spark our most intense feelings. These triggers, often rooted in past experiences or fears, can catch us off guard, propelling us into reactions that might not align with our intentions or values. To navigate this, consider:

- Keep a mood diary for a few weeks, noting instances when emotions felt particularly intense. Include details about what happened right before you noticed this shift in feeling.

- Reflect on patterns that emerge from your diary entries. Do certain situations, words, or people consistently precede these intense emotions?
- Contemplate the deeper fears or experiences connected to these triggers. Understanding the root can offer insights into why your emotions surface in the way they do.

This recognition is your map, helping to predict and prepare for emotional fluctuations before they lead you astray.

Breathing and Grounding Techniques

In moments when emotions threaten to capsize your calm, breathing and grounding techniques can serve as anchors, bringing you back to a state of equilibrium. These techniques are practical tools that can be employed anywhere, providing immediate relief:

- Focused Breathing: This technique involves taking slow, deep breaths and concentrating on each inhalation and exhalation. Imagine your breath as a wave, bringing calm with each cycle.
- The 5-4-3-2-1 Technique: Ground yourself by identifying five things you can see, four you can touch, three you can hear, two you can smell, and one you can taste. This method brings your attention to the present, diverting it from overwhelming emotions.

These techniques are like lifelines, capable of pulling you back from the edge of emotional overwhelm, offering a moment to regather and reassess.

Long-Term Emotional Management

While immediate techniques provide relief in the heat of the moment, cultivating a landscape of emotional stability requires long-term strategies. Often, this involves:

- Regular Therapy Sessions: Engaging with a therapist can offer deeper insights into your emotional world and equip you with personalized strategies for regulation.
- Mindfulness Practice: Incorporating mindfulness into your daily routine encourages a habit of present-moment awareness, reducing the intensity of emotional reactions over time.
- Emotional Literacy: Enhancing your understanding of different emotions and their nuances can help accurately identify your feelings, making it easier to address specific emotions rather than being overwhelmed by a vague sense of distress.

These strategies are akin to cultivating a garden; with regular care and attention, you can grow a landscape of emotional resilience that stands firm in the face of life's storms.

Differentiating Between Feelings and Reality

A crucial skill in emotional regulation is learning to differentiate between the immediate intensity of our feelings and the actual reality of the situation. This skill can prevent us from being swept away by emotional tsunamis, enabling us to respond rather than react. To develop this skill:

- Pause and Assess: When emotions surge, permit yourself to pause. Ask, "What am I feeling right now, and what is actually happening?" The pause can help you see if your emotional response is proportionate to the situation.
- Seek Perspective: Sometimes, discussing your feelings with a trusted friend or therapist can offer an outside perspective, helping to separate feelings from facts.
- Challenge Catastrophizing: If you imagine the worst-case scenario, challenge this by asking how likely it will happen. Reminding yourself of past instances when you've coped successfully can also help recalibrate your emotional response.

By practicing these skills, you can navigate your emotional world more confidently and clearly, ensuring that your feelings inform but don't control your actions. Emotional regulation, like any skill, grows stronger with practice. It's about setting a course through the waves of our feelings, steering with awareness and compassion, both for ourselves and others.

5.4 THE ART OF SELF-COMPASSION: BEING KIND TO YOUR INNER CHILD

Self-compassion is the gentle acknowledgment of one's suffering and an authentic desire to alleviate it. It's a nurturing presence for oneself, especially when navigating the complexities of anxious attachment. This nurturing attitude towards oneself can significantly shift how we relate to our past pains and current vulnerabilities.

Understanding Self-Compassion

At its core, self-compassion involves treating oneself with the same kindness, concern, and support that we would offer a good friend. It recognizes that imperfection and difficulties are part of the shared human experience. For individuals grappling with anxious attachment, cultivating self-compassion can be a transformative process, allowing them to approach their fears and insecurities with empathy rather than judgment. This approach fosters an environment where healing can commence and true self-acceptance can flourish.

Connecting with Your Inner Child

The "inner child" concept represents our original, authentic self, including all our past experiences and emotions, both joyful and painful. For many, the inner child holds the key to understanding the roots of anxious attachment. To connect with and offer compassion to your inner child:

- Visualization: Find a quiet space and close your eyes. Picture yourself as a child. Try to remember a time when you felt vulnerable or scared. What did you need most at that moment?
- Letter Writing: Write a letter to your younger self. Offer words of comfort, assurance, and encouragement. Acknowledge their fears and reassure them of their worth and the love that awaits them.
- Nurturing Activities: Engage in activities that you enjoyed as a child, whether that be drawing, playing outside, or listening to a favorite piece of music. Allow yourself to experience joy and curiosity through your inner child's eyes.

These exercises foster a deep connection with your inner child, enabling you to address and soothe past hurts and needs with compassion and understanding.

Practicing Self-Kindness

Incorporating self-kindness into daily life is an antidote to the self-criticism and judgment that often accompany anxious attachment. To practice self-kindness:

- Positive Self-Talk: Pay attention to the dialogue you have with yourself. When you notice self-criticism, pause and reframe the thought in a kinder, more supportive way.
- Self-Care Rituals: Create rituals that promote well-being and relaxation—a warm bath, a nature walk, or a hobby that brings you joy. Make these activities non-negotiable parts of your routine.
- Gratitude for Self: At the end of each day, write down three things you appreciate about yourself. Focus on qualities independent of external validation, such as resilience, creativity, or empathy.

Practicing self-kindness is a commitment to honoring and caring for oneself, recognizing that self-care is not selfish but essential for emotional health and well-being.

Forgiveness and Moving Forward

Forgiveness, both of oneself and others, plays a crucial role in the journey toward secure attachment. It's about releasing the hold that past mistakes and hurts have on us, allowing space for growth and new experiences. To embrace forgiveness:

- Self-Forgiveness: Acknowledge that making mistakes is part of being human. Reflect on past errors with understanding, focusing on the lessons learned rather than the pain caused.

- Forgiving Others: Consider how holding onto resentment and anger impacts your emotional health. Contemplate the act of forgiveness as a gift to yourself, a release from these burdens.
- Letting Go: Practice letting go of grievances through meditation, visualization, or writing. Imagine yourself releasing these weights, feeling lighter and more open to the present and future connections.

Forgiveness is not a denial of pain or an excuse for harmful behavior but a step towards emotional freedom and deeper self-compassion. It's a recognition that holding onto past hurts only limits our capacity for joy and connection.

Nurturing self-compassion and kindness, connecting with our inner child, and embracing forgiveness create a foundation of emotional resilience. This foundation supports us in navigating the vulnerabilities of anxious attachment with grace and empathy, fostering a sense of security and acceptance within ourselves. Through these practices, we learn to offer ourselves the compassion and understanding we so readily extend to others, acknowledging our worthiness of love and belonging.

5.5 MINDFULNESS AND PRESENCE: STAYING GROUNDED IN RELATIONSHIPS

Staying attuned to the present moment enriches our connections with others, allowing us to engage more deeply and authentically. Mindfulness, the practice of being fully present and engaged in the now without being overly reactive or overwhelmed by what's happening around us, offers a wealth of benefits for nurturing relationships. This approach fosters a profound emotional awareness that can enhance our interactions and elevate our communication, making each moment with our partners more meaningful.

Benefits of Mindfulness

Practicing mindfulness brings about a heightened emotional awareness that is a foundation for solid relationships. It encourages a deeper appreciation for the nuances of our partner's emotions, fostering empathy and understanding. Heightened awareness also aids in recognizing our emotional responses, providing clarity that can prevent misunderstandings and foster genuine connection. Moreover, mindfulness helps reduce stress and anxiety, common culprits that can cloud our judgment and negatively impact our relationships.

Mindfulness Practices

Incorporating mindfulness into our daily lives doesn't require extensive time commitments or special equipment. Here are a few simple practices:

- Mindful Breathing: Take a few minutes each day to focus solely on your breath. Breathwork can be done anywhere, anytime, and serves as a quick way to center yourself in the present.
- Mindful Listening: During conversations, focus entirely on what your partner is saying without planning your response. Your undivided attention shows respect and appreciation for their perspective, enhancing mutual understanding.
- Mindful Eating: Share meals with your partner where you both focus on the experience of eating—savoring the flavors, textures, and the act of sharing time together.

These practices can seamlessly integrate into daily routines, enhancing relationship satisfaction by fostering a shared sense of presence and appreciation for the little moments.

Staying Present in Interactions

Active interaction engagement requires conscious effort, especially in an age where distractions are plentiful. Techniques for staying present include:

- Eye Contact: Maintaining eye contact during conversations shows your partner that you are fully engaged and value the interaction.
- Device-Free Time: Allocate periods where you and your partner put away electronic devices, ensuring your time together is uninterrupted.
- Expressive Acknowledgment: Regularly affirm your partner's feelings and thoughts through verbal acknowledgments or physical gestures, reinforcing your engagement and presence in the conversation.

These strategies improve communication and reinforce the bond between you and your partner, making each interaction more meaningful.

Managing Anxiety in the Moment

Anxiety, particularly in moments of uncertainty or conflict, can disrupt our ability to stay present and connected. To manage stress and remain grounded:

- Recognize the Signs: Learn to identify your early signs of anxiety. Signs could be a racing heart, shallow breathing, or restlessness.

- Pause and Breathe: Before reacting, take a moment to pause. Focus on deep, slow breaths to help calm your mind and body.
- Focus on Sensory Experiences: Ground yourself by focusing on tactile sensations, such as the feel of your feet on the ground or the texture of an object in your hand. Mindfulness can help redirect your focus from anxiety to the present moment.
- Communicate Openly: If you feel overwhelmed, calmly communicate this to your partner. Sharing your experience can help them understand your needs and provide support.

Adopting these techniques allows us to navigate moments of anxiety with grace, ensuring that our relationships remain a source of support and connection, even when faced with challenges.

As we conclude this exploration of mindfulness and presence in relationships, we're reminded of the power of staying anchored in the present. The practices outlined here, from mindful breathing to active listening and managing anxiety, serve as tools to enhance our connections, making every interaction with our partners richer and more fulfilling. They encourage us to appreciate the beauty of the present moment, deepening our relationships and fostering a sense of shared understanding and intimacy. Let's carry these insights with us as we move forward, allowing them to guide us in nurturing our relationships with mindfulness, presence, and compassion.

please take a moment to share your review!

Hello Dear Reader,

We're halfway through our journey in "Overcoming Anxious Attachment," and I hope you're finding the insights and tools helpful as you navigate your path to emotional freedom and confidence. Your thoughts and experiences with the book are incredibly valuable, and I would love to hear from you!

Please take a moment to share your review. Your feedback helps others discover the benefits of understanding and overcoming anxious attachment. Here are a few questions to get you started:

1. **What chapter or section resonated with you the most?**
2. **How has this book helped you in your journey so far?**
3. **What new insights have you gained about anxious attachment?**
4. **Are there any particular exercises or practices that you found especially helpful?**

Your honest review will not only support me as an author but also guide others who are looking for ways to build stronger, more secure relationships.

Thank you for being a part of this journey. Your courage and dedication to understanding yourself better are truly inspiring!

Simply scan the QR code below to leave your review:

Thank you from the bottom of my heart,

Kelly

nurturing connection through communication

I magine a dance with two people moving in harmony, each step and turn perfectly in sync. Much like communication in relationships, this dance requires understanding, attentiveness, and a willingness to move together. In this dance, we find the rhythm of connection and a stronger beat when we learn to express ourselves clearly and listen with intention. In this chapter, we'll unravel the threads of effective communication, turning potential discord into a symphony of mutual understanding and respect.

Expressing Emotional Needs

Expressing emotional needs isn't about laying out a list of demands but sharing parts of your inner world with someone you trust. It's saying, "When you hug me after a long day, it makes me feel valued and loved," instead of a vague "I wish you were more affectionate." Here's how to do it:

- Be Specific: Instead of "I need more attention," try "I love it when we talk over dinner without our phones. Can we do that more often?"
- Timing Matters: Choose a calm, neutral time for these conversations. Right after a disagreement or when someone is rushing out the door isn't ideal.
- I Statements: "I feel…" is less about blaming and more about owning your feelings. It's saying, "I feel lonely when we don't spend time together," rather than "You never spend time with me."

Understanding Partner's Communication Style

Everyone has a unique way of expressing themselves. Some prefer direct conversation, while others find comfort in writing a thoughtful letter or email. Recognizing and adapting to your partner's style can make all the difference. For instance, if your partner processes their thoughts better in writing, giving them space to pen down their feelings before a verbal discussion can lead to more meaningful exchanges. It's about finding a middle ground where both feel heard and respected.

Active Expression and Receptive Listening

This dance of communication is a two-way street, balancing talking and listening. Active expression means sharing your thoughts and feelings openly, not just with words but through your body language and actions. Conversely, receptive listening is truly hearing what your partner is saying without immediately formulating a response or judgment. It involves:

- Eye Contact: Shows you're fully engaged.
- Body Language: Nodding and leaning in slightly can signal your attention.

- Reflective Responses: Phrases like "What I'm hearing is…" or "It sounds like you're feeling…" validate your partner's feelings and clarify understanding.

Feedback Loops

Feedback loops are about giving and receiving information on how actions or words are perceived, creating a cycle of growth and understanding. After expressing a need or concern, ask for your partner's perspective and be open to their feedback. Example:

- After sharing something important, you could ask, "How does that make you feel?" or "I'd love to know your thoughts on this."
- When your partner shares their feelings, follow up with, "Do you feel like I understand what you're sharing?" or "Is there more you'd like me to know?"

These feedback loops deepen understanding and reinforce the connection, ensuring both partners feel valued and heard.

At its heart, communication is the thread that weaves the tapestry of our relationships, colored by our words, shaped by our listening, and strengthened by our willingness to connect authentically. As we navigate this dance together, let's remember that it's not about perfection but progress, not about always being in sync but finding our way back to each other, step by step.

6.2 SETTING BOUNDARIES WITH LOVE AND RESPECT

In the dance of relationships, boundaries are the steps that keep us from stepping on each other's toes. They are not walls meant to distance us but guides that help us move together harmoniously. Recognizing their role in maintaining self-respect and the health of our relationships is the first step toward a more balanced and fulfilling partnership.

Boundaries express our values, needs, and relationship goals. They enable us to honor our self-worth while respecting our partners' autonomy. When clearly defined and mutually respected, boundaries can prevent misunderstandings and resentment, paving the way for deeper intimacy and trust.

Identifying Personal Boundaries

Understanding your boundaries begins with deep diving into your values and needs. Reflect on what matters most to you in a relationship and what you consider non-negotiable, from needing personal space to how you make decisions together. Consider the following steps to clarify your boundaries:

- Reflect on past relationships, noting situations where you felt uncomfortable or upset. These instances often highlight boundary violations. Imagine your ideal relationship dynamics. What behaviors or situations are deal-breakers for you?
- Differentiate between flexible boundaries that can adapt to circumstances and rigid boundaries that are fundamental to your well-being.

Communicating Boundaries

Once you've identified your boundaries, sharing them with your partner is crucial. Clear, assertive, and respectful communication ensures your message is heard without causing defensiveness. Here are strategies to effectively communicate your boundaries:

- Choose a calm moment to discuss your boundaries, avoiding times of stress or conflict.
- Use clear, concise language. For example, instead of saying, "I don't like it when you interrupt me," try, "I feel valued when I can finish my thoughts without interruption."
- Explain the rationale behind your boundary. Understanding the 'why' can help your partner see the importance of respecting this boundary.
- Be open to discussion. Your partner may have different perspectives, and finding a compromise that honors both sets of needs is part of a healthy relationship.

Respecting and Enforcing Boundaries

Establishing boundaries is only half the equation; respecting and enforcing them completes it. Mutual respect for boundaries signifies a deep respect for each other's individuality and needs. Consider the following:

- When a boundary is communicated, take it seriously. Show respect by acknowledging and adhering to your partner's boundaries, and expect the same in return.
- If a boundary is crossed, address it promptly. Let your partner know that the boundary has been violated and discuss how to prevent it from happening again.
- Recognize that consistently disrespecting boundaries is a red flag. It may indicate underlying issues in the relationship that need to be addressed with professional help.

Similarly, if you find your boundaries being repeatedly ignored or violated, it's essential to enforce them. Enforcing boundaries entails reiterating your needs, seeking support from a therapist, or reevaluating the relationship. Remember, boundaries are a form of self-care, and upholding them is crucial to your emotional well-being.

Setting boundaries with love and respect is not about creating distance but building relationships where both partners feel seen, valued, and respected. It's a delicate balance that requires ongoing communication, flexibility, and a deep commitment to each other's happiness and growth. Through this process, we transform boundaries from mere lines that shouldn't be crossed into bridges that connect us more deeply to those we love.

6.3 NAVIGATING CONFLICT WITH CONFIDENCE

Conflict, often seen as a storm cloud looming over relationships, holds the potential for rejuvenating rain, nourishing growth, and deeper connection. It's a natural part of any relationship, signaling areas where understanding and compromise can bloom. Conflicts can transform into opportunities to strengthen the bond between partners when approached with confidence and constructive intent.

A New Perspective on Conflict

Viewing conflict through a lens of growth rather than dread shifts the dynamic from adversarial to collaborative. It recognizes that disagreements are not battlefields but classrooms where we learn about each other's needs and fears and how to support one another more effectively. This perspective encourages openness and curiosity, inviting questions like, "What can we discover about each other through this?" and "How can we grow from this experience?"

Strategies for Healthy Conflict Resolution

Healthy conflict resolution is finding a path that respects both partners' needs and perspectives. The following strategies lay the groundwork for resolving conflicts constructively:

- Identify the Core Issue: What sparks a conflict is often not the real issue. Uncovering the underlying concern can shift the conversation from surface symptoms to root causes.
- Speak Your Truth with Kindness: Share your feelings and thoughts honestly but with care for your partner's feelings. It's possible to be truthful without being hurtful.
- Seek to Understand Before Being Understood: Give your partner the space to share their story. Listening to understand rather than to respond fosters empathy and bridges gaps in perception.
- Focus on Solutions, Not Blame: Shift the dialogue towards finding solutions that work for both of you. Asking, "What do we need to move forward?" emphasizes collaborative problem-solving.

Techniques for De-escalating Conflict

When emotions run high, stepping back from the brink of escalation can prevent hurtful words and actions that might be regretted later. Consider these de-escalation techniques:

- Take a Breather: If tension escalates, pausing the conversation can help. Agreeing to take a short break lets both partners cool down and collect their thoughts.
- Use Humor Wisely: A light-hearted comment or gentle humor can sometimes break the tension, as long as it doesn't hurt your partner's feelings.

- Acknowledge Emotions: Recognizing and acknowledging your partner's feelings can diffuse defensiveness. Phrases like, "I see you're upset about this, and I understand why," validate emotions without escalating the conflict.

The Value of Learning from Conflict

Each conflict holds lessons on how to love and support each other better. Reflecting on conflicts after the resolution can prevent the repetition of hurtful patterns and deepen mutual understanding. Consider these reflective practices:

- Discuss What Worked: After resolving a conflict, discuss what strategies or approaches helped, thus reinforcing positive communication patterns for future disagreements.
- Identify Triggers: Understanding what triggers emotional responses in each other can help avoid unnecessary conflicts and foster a more supportive environment.
- Express Appreciation: Acknowledging each other's efforts to resolve the conflict strengthens the relationship and builds resilience for future challenges.

Navigating conflict with confidence doesn't mean avoiding disagreements or suppressing emotions. It's about embracing disputes as opportunities to learn, grow, and understand each other more deeply. With the proper perspective and tools, conflicts can become catalysts for strengthening the bond between partners, turning storm clouds into nourishing rain that promotes growth and connection.

6.4 THE POWER OF ACTIVE LISTENING

Active listening is more than simply hearing the words spoken by another; it's an intentional effort to comprehend the complete message shared, both verbally and non-verbally. This skill is pivotal in nurturing deep, meaningful connections, allowing us to understand our partners fully and, in turn, be understood. Within the dance of dialogue, active listening is the step that ensures we move in harmony, preventing missteps of miscommunication and misunderstandings.

Elements of Active Listening

Active listening is composed of several key elements that, when combined, facilitate a profound level of communication:

- Non-verbal Cues: Observing body language, facial expressions, and eye contact gives insight into unspoken feelings and attitudes. A nod or a gentle lean towards the speaker signals engagement and encourages further sharing.
- Reflective Responding: This involves paraphrasing or summarizing the speaker's words to confirm understanding. It's akin to holding up a mirror to the speaker's words, reflecting them for validation and clarity.
- Empathy and Patience: Empathy involves recognizing and acknowledging the speaker's emotions without judgment. Patience allows the speaker to express thoughts and feelings fully without feeling rushed or dismissed.
- Clarifying Questions: Asking open-ended questions about the speaker's message helps to clarify any ambiguity and demonstrates a genuine interest in understanding their perspective.

Improving Empathy Through Listening

Empathy grows in the soil of active listening. By fully attending to our partner's words and emotions, we view situations and feelings from their vantage point. This deep level of understanding fosters a compassionate connection, making it easier to navigate the complexities of relationships with sensitivity and kindness. Empathy, nurtured through active listening, acts as a bridge, connecting disparate islands of experience into a cohesive understanding.

Practicing Active Listening

Integrating active listening into daily interactions can transform the quality of communication in relationships. Here are practical exercises to enhance active listening skills:

- The Listening Mirror: Spend a day reflecting on what your partner says during conversations. Aim to paraphrase their statements accurately, asking for feedback on your reflections to ensure you've understood correctly.
- Silent Moments: Allocate periods where you listen without the intent to reply. Focus solely on understanding your partner's perspective, resisting the urge to formulate responses until they fully express themselves.
- Emotion Spotting: During conversations, identify the emotions behind your partner's words. Afterward, share your observations and ask if you've understood their feelings accurately.

Overcoming Barriers to Listening

Several common barriers can hinder effective listening. Recognizing and addressing these obstacles is crucial for fostering open, empathetic communication:

- Distractions: In our digitally-driven world, distractions are abundant. Prioritize conversations by setting aside electronic devices and choosing settings free from interruptions.
- Preconceived Notions: Entering conversations with preconceived ideas about what your partner will say can block genuine understanding. Approach each dialogue with an open mind, ready to be surprised.
- Interrupting: Cutting off your partner disrupts the flow of communication and signals that your response is more important than their message. Practice patience, allowing your partner to complete their thoughts fully before responding.
- Emotional Reactions: Strong emotional reactions can cloud our ability to listen. If a conversation triggers intense feelings, it may be necessary to take a moment to calm down before continuing the dialogue.

Active listening is more than a technique; it's a gift we offer to those we care about. It says, "Your thoughts and feelings matter to me." Improving our active listening skills enhances our relationships and cultivates a more profound connection and understanding with those around us. Through deliberate active listening, we ensure that our conversations are not just exchanges of words but meaningful interactions that enrich our relationships and lives.

6.5 ASKING FOR WHAT YOU NEED WITHOUT FEAR

Communicating our desires and requirements to those we love can sometimes feel like navigating a tightrope. On one side, there's the fear of rejection or criticism, a chasm that seems to widen with every unspoken word. On the other, the solid ground of understanding and connection awaits, but only if we dare to walk the line. Overcoming these fears and adopting assertive yet gentle ways of expressing our needs bridges this gap and fortifies the ties that bind us to our loved ones.

Overcoming Fear of Rejection

The apprehension that our needs, once voiced, will not be met with understanding but with rejection or criticism can silence even the most urgent pleas for connection. This fear, while deeply rooted in our instinctual aversion to rejection, can be assuaged. Start by acknowledging the validity of your needs. Recognize that having needs doesn't make you burdensome or needy; it makes you human. Next, remind yourself of your worth, independent of anyone's approval or acceptance. This internal reassurance is your safety net, softening the fear of falling.

Strategies for Assertive Requesting

Assertiveness, the ability to express your thoughts and feelings confidently and calmly, is vital to effectively communicating your needs. Here are some strategies to help you ask for what you need without fear:

- Practice in Low-Stakes Situations: Start small. Practice being assertive in situations where the stakes aren't high.
- Use "I" Statements: Frame your requests from your perspective to avoid sounding accusatory. For example, "I feel valued when we spend quality time together" instead of "You never spend time with me."
- Be Clear and Specific: Ambiguity can lead to misunderstandings. Clearly state what you need, why it's important to you, and how it can be achieved.

Building a Supportive Dialogue

A supportive dialogue is one in which both partners feel safe expressing their needs and are confident they will be met with empathy and understanding. Cultivating this environment requires patience, practice, and a commitment to mutual respect. Encourage open communication by regularly checking in, actively listening, and validating each other's feelings. Remember, it's not about agreeing on everything but understanding and respecting each other's perspectives.

Self-Respect and Mutual Respect

At the heart of asking for what you need lies a deep-seated respect for yourself and the person you ask. Recognizing that your needs are valid and deserving of attention is a fundamental act of self-respect. Similarly, approaching your partner with the belief that they can understand and meet your needs expresses respect for them. This mutual respect is the fertile ground where the seeds of a healthy, robust relationship can grow.

In navigating the delicate balance of expressing our needs, we discover the strength of our voice and the depth of our connections. By overcoming the fear of rejection, embracing assertiveness, fostering supportive dialogue, and grounding our requests in mutual respect, we pave the way for a relationship that thrives on understanding and empathy. As we close this chapter, let us carry forward the knowledge that asking for what we need, far from pushing others away, draws us closer to the ones we love, strengthening the bonds of trust and affection that bind us.

As we move forward, we remember that our relationships are ever-evolving tapestries woven from countless threads of interaction, communication, and shared experiences. Each request we make, each need we express, adds color and texture to this tapestry, enriching our connections and deepening our understanding of one another.

paths to healing: embracing support and strategy

Imagine you're lost in a dense forest. It's easy to feel overwhelmed by the towering trees and the myriad paths that lead in all directions. Now, think of therapy as finding a guide who knows the woods well. They can't walk the path for you, but they can offer insights, suggest directions, and help you see the forest in a way that suddenly makes sense. This chapter is about finding that guide, choosing your path, and taking those crucial steps toward the sunlight.

Professional Guidance: A Safe Space to Explore

Therapy offers a unique space just for you, a place where you're heard without judgment and supported with compassion. Here, you can lay bare your fears, dissect your anxieties, and get to the root of your attachment wounds. It's like having a beacon in the darkness, guiding you through the tangled undergrowth of your emotions and experiences.

- Why Therapy? Think of it as a partnership where the goal is your well-being. You bring your life's story, and your therapist brings their expertise in navigating emotional landscapes. This collaboration can illuminate patterns you might not see on your own, offering new perspectives on old problems.

Therapeutic Approaches: Finding What Fits

Just as different keys open different locks, various therapeutic approaches can unlock the healing process for different individuals. Cognitive-behavioral therapy (CBT) and emotionally focused therapy (EFT) are two approaches that have shown promise for those grappling with anxious attachment.

- CBT: This method is like rearranging a cluttered room. It helps you identify and challenge the distorted thought patterns contributing to your anxious attachment, replacing them with more balanced and realistic ones. It's practical, focused on the here and now, and provides tools you can use outside the therapy session.
- EFT: Imagine dancing to a song that stirs deep emotions. EFT taps into the power of emotions, using them as the entry point for healing. It's beneficial for couples, helping you and your partner create a more secure bond by understanding and responding to each other's deep emotional needs.

Personalized Strategy: Tailoring the Approach

No two forests are the same; similarly, your path through emotional healing is unique. A personalized therapeutic strategy considers your history, strengths, struggles, and goals. It's a map drawn just for you.

- Crafting Your Map: Your therapist might start with broad strokes, outlining the general direction. As you move forward, these lines become more defined, becoming a clear path tailored to your needs. Specific exercises, homework assignments, or experimenting with new ways of relating to yourself and others are all part of the process.

Commitment to Process: The Road Takes Time

Healing, especially from wounds as deep as those caused by anxious attachment, is not instantaneous. It's a process, often slow and sometimes challenging. Committing to this process is committing to yourself and believing you deserve to heal, grow, and find peace.

- Patience and Perseverance: Some days, it might feel like you're making huge strides. Other days, it might seem like you're back at square one. Both are part of the healing journey. Remember, every step, even those that feel like setbacks, moves you forward.

This chapter isn't just about therapy's role in healing attachment wounds. It's about recognizing that sometimes, finding our way through the forest of our fears and anxieties requires a guide, a strategy, and a commitment to keep walking, even when the path feels uncertain. With the right support, a tailored approach, and dedication to the process, the journey can lead to profound growth and healing.

7.2 BUILDING A SUPPORT NETWORK: FINDING YOUR TRIBE

The significance of weaving a fabric of connections with friends, family, and peers who genuinely grasp and uplift your emotional development cannot be overstressed. Imagine these connections as threads in a safety net, each strand strengthening your resilience and providing a cushion of support for those moments when the ground seems to vanish beneath your feet.

Community Importance

The tapestry of human connection underscores a profound truth about our nature: we are inherently social beings, thriving on interaction and mutual understanding. A robust support network acts not just as a sounding board for our fears and aspirations but also as a mirror reflecting the multifaceted dimensions of our journey. In the midst of shared experiences and empathetic ears, it's here that we find validation, encouragement, and, sometimes, the tough love necessary to push through barriers.

- The relief of discovering you're not alone in your struggles is immeasurable. It provides both comfort and a shared sense of purpose.

Seeking Supportive Environments

In the quest for environments that resonate with our needs, it's crucial to venture beyond our comfort zones. Support groups and online communities offer havens where experiences and coping strategies can be freely exchanged. These spaces often serve as lifelines, offering perspective and advice grounded in lived experiences.

- Initiating this search might begin with a simple online query or reaching out to mental health professionals for recommendations. The key is to remain open to different formats, whether they're in-person meetings or virtual forums.

Mutual Support

Extending support to others can be a powerful catalyst in your healing process. It's a dynamic exchange, with the act of giving providing as much benefit as receiving. Through this reciprocal arrangement, we deepen our understanding of our own experiences and gain a sense of purpose and contribution.

- Volunteering as a mentor for those newly navigating the waters of anxious attachment or simply offering an empathetic ear can reinforce your insights and strengthen your resolve.

Boundaries and Support

While the value of a support network is undeniable, establishing healthy boundaries within these relationships is crucial. Boundaries ensure that the support received and given does not encroach upon personal space or become a source of dependency.

- Communicating your needs and limits clearly and respecting those of others ensures that these relationships remain healthy and supportive. It's about finding the balance between being open to receiving help and maintaining your autonomy.

The steps in the intricate dance of building and nurturing a support network seem daunting at first. Yet, with each connection forged, each conversation shared, and each boundary respected, the dance becomes less about the steps and more about the flow. In this flow, we find our tribe, a collective of souls who walk with us, reminding us that no matter how solitary our path might feel, we never truly walk alone.

7.3 THE HEALING POWER OF JOURNALING

In the quiet moments when we find ourselves alone with our thoughts, a blank page in a journal offers a canvas for self-expression, a space where the heart's whispers and soul's cries can be acknowledged and explored. Journaling, an age-old practice, stands today as a potent tool in the quest for emotional clarity and healing. It serves as a mirror, reflecting our innermost thoughts and feelings, allowing us to sift through the layers of our consciousness to uncover the roots of our anxious attachment and gently guide ourselves toward growth.

Self-Reflection Tool

Imagine journaling as a key that unlocks the door to your inner world, revealing patterns of thought and behavior that often go unnoticed. In writing, we voice our fears, hopes, and the intricate web of emotions that define our experiences of attachment and connection. This introspective practice offers a unique opportunity to pause, look inward, and truly listen to ourselves, providing insights that can illuminate the path to healing.

- Through reflective writing, you can trace the lineage of your anxious attachment, from its earliest origins to its present manifestations, uncovering how past experiences shape your current relational dynamics.
- Journaling also allows you to document your emotional fluctuations, offering a tangible way to track your progress

over time. You can identify triggers that exacerbate your anxiety and celebrate moments of breakthrough and resilience.

Journal Prompts

To guide your exploration and deepen your journaling practice, consider engaging with the following prompts:

- Describe a moment when you felt overwhelmed by anxious attachment. What were the circumstances? What thoughts and emotions surfaced?
- Reflect on a relationship where your anxious attachment was particularly pronounced. How did it impact your interactions? What patterns can you identify?
- Write a letter to your younger self, offering compassion and understanding for the moments when anxious attachment first took root.
- Envision a future where you've moved beyond anxious attachment. What does it look like? How do you feel in your relationships?

These prompts are starting points, invitations to delve into the complexities of your emotional world. They can be revisited and expanded upon, each entry building on the last to create a rich tapestry of self-awareness and insight.

Regular Practice

Incorporating journaling into your daily routine transforms it from a sporadic activity into a powerful ritual for self-care and emotional processing. Set aside a few minutes each day, perhaps in the morning, to set the tone for the day ahead or in the evening as a reflective practice before bed. This consistent engagement with your thoughts and feelings can act as a gentle form of therapy, offering relief, fostering self-compassion, and encouraging emotional growth.

- Find a quiet, comfortable space where you can write without interruptions. This physical setting can signal your mind that it's time for introspection and healing.
- Don't worry about grammar or spelling. The focus is on expression, not perfection. Let your thoughts and emotions flow freely onto the page.

Privacy and Honesty

The true power of journaling lies in its capacity to be utterly private, a sacred space where honesty reigns supreme. Here, you can express your deepest fears, darkest thoughts, and most fervent hopes without concern for judgment or misunderstanding. This level of candor enables journaling to be such a transformative tool.

- Treat your journal as a trusted confidant with whom you can share anything and everything. This openness paves the way for genuine self-discovery and healing.
- Consider keeping your journal in a secure location. Knowing that your reflections are private can encourage greater honesty in your writing.

In this quiet dialogue with the self, journaling becomes more than just a method for processing emotions; it evolves into a journey of self-discovery, a way to navigate the complexities of anxious attachment with grace and insight. Through writing, we can uncover hidden fears, celebrate personal growth, and gradually move towards a place of greater emotional freedom and security.

7.4 RECLAIMING YOUR STORY: NARRATIVE THERAPY BASICS

Narrative therapy opens the door to exploring how we perceive and narrate our experiences, particularly those that have shaped our anxious attachment styles. This therapeutic approach rests on the idea that we are not our problems; rather, our problems are separate from us, woven into the stories we tell ourselves about who we are. At the heart of narrative therapy is the empowering realization that we can edit, revise, and change these stories, altering our relationship with our problems and ourselves.

Narrative Therapy Introduction

Introducing narrative therapy, it's akin to discovering a new lens through which to view your life's story. This lens lets you observe your experiences from a distance, providing clarity and objectivity. The fundamental belief here is that the stories we tell ourselves about our lives significantly influence how we perceive our identities and tackle our problems. By identifying and understanding these narratives, narrative therapy offers a path to rewriting them in ways that foster empowerment and healing.

Authoring Your Life

Seeing yourself as the author of your story is both liberating and daunting. It suggests that, despite past chapters being written under the influence of anxious attachment, the pen is now in your hand, and the pages ahead are blank, waiting for your words. This shift in perspective encourages a proactive stance towards life, where you are in control and capable of crafting a narrative that aligns with your aspirations and values. It's about moving from a position of feeling acted upon by your anxious attachment to acting intentionally, authoring a life story that reflects resilience and secure attachment.

Identifying Dominant Narratives

The stories that profoundly impact our lives and relationships often operate just below the surface of our consciousness. These dominant narratives can include beliefs like "I am not enough" or "Love is conditional." To identify these narratives:

- Pay close attention to recurring themes in your thoughts and conversations about relationships and self-worth.
- Notice the emotions these thoughts evoke, as they often signal areas where dominant narratives are at play.
- Reflect on the origins of these stories. Many are inherited from family, past relationships, or societal messages.

Acknowledging these narratives is the first step in challenging their hold on your life. It allows you to question their validity and explore alternative stories that offer a more empowering and balanced view of yourself and your capacity for healthy relationships.

Rewriting the Script

Once dominant narratives are brought to light, the process of rewriting begins. This doesn't mean denying your past experiences but reframing them to highlight your agency, strengths, and the possibility of change. Strategies for rewriting your life script include:

- Identify Counter-Narratives: For every disempowering story you've told yourself, there's a counter-narrative waiting to be discovered. If your dominant narrative is "My needs always drive people away," a counter-narrative could be "Expressing my needs helps me build deeper, more authentic connections."

- Collect Evidence: Gather instances from your past and present that support your counter-narratives. These can be moments of resilience, times when you were loved and accepted for who you are, or instances where expressing your needs led to positive outcomes.
- Embrace Complexity: Recognize that your story, like all great stories, contains multitudes. It's filled with triumphs and setbacks, laughter and tears. Embracing the complexity of your experiences allows for a richer, more nuanced narrative that acknowledges your growth and potential.
- Seek Feedback: Share your new narratives with trusted friends, family, or your therapist. Their perspectives can offer validation and insights that reinforce your rewritten script.

Engaging in narrative therapy is akin to taking a step back, examining the tapestry of your life, and realizing that you have the threads in your hand. You can weave patterns of resilience, empowerment, and secure attachment into the fabric of your story. This realization is transformative, providing a foundation for building a narrative that supports healing and growth.

7.5 SELF-HELP RESOURCES: BOOKS, PODCASTS, AND WORKSHOPS

In a world brimming with information, sifting through to find the gems that resonate with our experiences of anxious attachment can feel overwhelming. Yet, the right book, podcast, or workshop can light up our understanding of ourselves and our relationships in ways we hadn't anticipated. Here, we'll explore a selection of these resources, why they matter, and how actively engaging with them can shape our paths to healing.

Curated Recommendations

Navigating the sea of available self-help resources, I've handpicked a selection that stands out for their depth, accessibility, and transformative potential. These recommendations are not just about understanding anxious attachment; they are about moving beyond it.

- Books: Look for titles that blend scientific research with personal narratives, offering insight and relatability. Books that provide practical exercises or strategies for managing anxious attachment are particularly valuable, as they bridge the gap between theory and practice.
- Podcasts: There are several insightful series where hosts delve into the nuances of attachment theories, often featuring interviews with experts in psychology and relationship counseling. These can be a great way to absorb information during your commute or downtime.
- Workshops: Interactive workshops, whether online or in-person, offer a dynamic environment for learning. These sessions often include role-playing, group discussions, and personal reflection activities, making the learning experience engaging and deeply personal.

Diverse Perspectives

One of the strengths of exploring a variety of self-help resources is the exposure to various perspectives and methodologies. This diversity enriches our understanding, allowing us to approach our healing from multiple angles. It teaches us that there is no one-size-fits-all solution to overcoming anxious attachment; instead, it's about finding the blend of approaches that speaks to us personally.

- Engaging with authors and speakers from different backgrounds and disciplines can broaden our horizons and introduce us to new strategies and insights we might not have considered otherwise.

Active Engagement

To truly benefit from these resources, passive consumption isn't enough. Active engagement means not just reading or listening but integrating what we learn into our daily lives.

- Taking Notes: Jot down insights, questions, and reflections as you go. This helps reinforce your learning and makes it easier to revisit key points later.
- Implementing Strategies: Put the techniques and exercises you come across into practice. Experiment with different approaches to see what resonates with you and what leads to noticeable changes in your thoughts, feelings, and behaviors.
- Reflecting on Progress: Periodically review your notes and reflections to assess your progress. Recognize patterns in what has been most helpful and consider how to build on these insights moving forward.

Community Learning

Participating in workshops or joining discussion groups around self-help books or podcasts can amplify the benefits of these resources. Sharing experiences and strategies with others navigating similar paths can provide support, validation, and a sense of connection. It reminds us that we're not alone in our struggles and that there's strength in community.

- These communal experiences can offer new perspectives and insights as participants share their journeys and what has worked for them.

In curating and engaging with these resources, we equip ourselves with a toolkit for understanding and navigating anxious attachment. From the insights gained through books and podcasts to the active learning and connection found in workshops, each resource offers a stepping stone on our path to healing. We can make meaningful strides toward emotional freedom and healthier relationships by approaching these materials with an open mind and a commitment to applying what we learn.

As we close this exploration of self-help resources, let's continue to understand that healing and growth are ongoing processes. The insights and strategies we've gathered are about overcoming anxious attachment and enriching our relationships with ourselves and others. With this foundation, we're better prepared to face the challenges and opportunities that lie ahead, moving forward with confidence and clarity.

CHAPTER 8

cultivating resilience

I magine you're watching a sunset, the sky a canvas of resilience. The sun dips below the horizon each evening, not as an act of surrender but as a promise to rise again. This natural cycle mirrors our capacity to face darkness and emerge with a renewed light. Resilience isn't about avoiding the night; it's about trusting in the following dawn. So, how do we fortify this trust within ourselves, especially when anxious attachment often clouds our skies?

8.1 BOUNCING BACK: BUILDING RESILIENCE THROUGH SETBACKS

Resilience Fundamentals

Resilience is that inner steel that allows us to rebound from setbacks or stress. It's not a trait that people either have or don't have. It involves behaviors, thoughts, and actions that anyone can learn and develop. For those wrestling with anxious attachment, resilience might seem like a distant concept, but it's closer than you think. It's in the small decisions to keep moving forward, the courage to open up again after being hurt, and the strength to believe in better days ahead.

Learning from Failure

Think about when a toddler learns to walk. They don't give up after the first fall. They get up, perhaps after a few tears, and try again, their determination unshaken. Similarly, setbacks and failures are not the universe's way of pointing out what we can't do but are, in fact, growth opportunities. The key is in how we respond:

- When a relationship doesn't work out, it's tempting to spiral into self-doubt. Instead, ask yourself, "What can I learn from this experience?"
- Failed attempts at changing attachment behaviors can be disheartening. Reflect on what didn't work and why, adjusting your approach accordingly.

Strategies for Resilience

Building emotional resilience is like constructing a fortress where your heart can safely weather storms. Here are some bricks for that fortress:

- Mindfulness: Practice being present. When anxiety about relationships tries to pull you into the past or future, ground yourself in the now. Simple breathing exercises can help center your thoughts.
- Positive Self-Talk: Change the narrative in your head. Instead of "I always mess up," try "I made a mistake, but I'm learning." Words have power, especially the ones we tell ourselves.

- Flexibility in Thinking: Adopt a flexible approach to problems. A relationship hiccup isn't a catastrophe but a chance to learn and adapt. Being open to different outcomes can alleviate anxiety.

Success Stories

Consider the story of someone who used their experiences as stepping stones after a series of tumultuous relationships. They started journaling to process their emotions, joined support groups to share and learn from others, and sought therapy to unravel their anxious attachment. Over time, they noticed a shift in how they viewed themselves and their relationships. This person's journey from a place of fear to one of strength and insight underscores that resilience is not just about bouncing back but also growing up.

When building resilience, remember that it's not about never falling but finding the courage to stand up each time, knowing that a sunrise follows each sunset.

8.2 THE ROLE OF PHYSICAL WELL-BEING IN EMOTIONAL HEALTH

In a world where the mind and body are often viewed as separate entities, it's crucial to recognize the intricate dance they perform together, influencing and shaping each other's states. This interplay becomes especially poignant when considering the impact of physical well-being on emotional resilience. The vitality of our body acts as a foundation upon which our emotional strength is built, enabling us to navigate the ebbs and flows of life with a steadier heart and a clearer mind.

Body-Mind Connection

At the core of our being, the body and mind are not just connected but profoundly intertwined. This relationship means physical health directly affects our emotional well-being and resilience. For instance, a body nourished and cared for becomes a vessel of strength, capable of supporting us through emotional turmoil. Conversely, when we neglect our physical health, our emotional resilience can waver, making us more susceptible to stress and anxiety. Acknowledging this connection opens the door to practices that honor and nurture our physical and emotional selves.

Physical Activity Benefits

Engaging in regular physical activity stands out as a powerful tool for enhancing mood and reducing stress levels. Moving our bodies through a brisk walk, a yoga session, or a dance class triggers a cascade of biochemical reactions. Endorphins, often dubbed the 'feel-good' hormones, are released, naturally lifting our spirits and providing a sense of calm. Moreover, physical activity helps regulate our sleep patterns and boost our self-esteem, further fortifying our emotional resilience. Consider these benefits a compelling reason to weave movement into the fabric of your daily routine.

- Mood Elevation: Just thirty minutes of moderate exercise can significantly uplift your mood.
- Stress Reduction: Regular physical activity lowers cortisol levels, the body's stress hormone.
- Enhanced Sleep: Physical activity during the day promotes restful sleep, which is crucial for emotional recovery and resilience.

Nutrition and Sleep

The fuel we provide our bodies and the rest we allow them significantly influence our emotional landscape. Balanced nutrition ensures our brain and body have the essential nutrients needed for optimal functioning, directly impacting our mood and stress resilience. For example, foods rich in omega-3 fatty acids support brain health and emotional well-being. Similarly, prioritizing sleep is not merely about rest but about giving our emotional selves the space to recover and regenerate. Adequate sleep is a buffer against stress and anxiety, providing a more robust platform to face challenges.

- Balanced Nutrition: Incorporating a variety of whole foods rich in vitamins, minerals, and antioxidants supports overall health and emotional stability.
- Adequate Sleep: Aim for 7-9 hours of quality sleep per night to support emotional and physical health.

Integrated Wellness Approach

Adopting an integrated approach to wellness acknowledges the multifaceted nature of our being, recognizing that the harmony between our physical, emotional, and mental health supports emotional resilience. This holistic perspective encourages practices that nourish every part of ourselves. It's about creating a lifestyle that values and attends to our physical well-being as a pillar of our emotional strength. From the food we eat to how we move and rest our bodies, each choice is a step toward a more resilient self.

To cultivate this integrated approach, consider incorporating the following into your life:

- Daily Movement: Find a form of physical activity you enjoy and make it a non-negotiable part of your day.
- Mindful Eating: Approach food with mindfulness, choosing nourishing options that fuel both body and mind.
- Restorative Sleep: Establish a calming bedtime routine to encourage quality sleep, understanding its critical role in emotional health.
- Reflection and Mindfulness: Pair physical activities with mindful reflection, using movement as a time to connect with yourself on a deeper level.

By honoring the bond between our physical and emotional selves, we enhance our capacity to face life's challenges and deepen our connection to the joy and beauty in our daily experiences. This integrated approach to wellness reminds us that caring for our bodies is not just an act of self-love but a foundational practice for building resilience and navigating life with grace and strength.

8.3 CULTIVATING JOY AND GRATITUDE IN EVERYDAY LIFE

In the tapestry of our lives, threads of joy and gratitude weave patterns of resilience, offering a counterbalance to the shadows of anxious attachment. These practices, grounded in the present, encourage us to recognize the abundance within our day-to-day existence, transforming our perception of the world and our place within it. Through intentional actions, we can illuminate our lives with moments of appreciation and happiness, fostering an environment where emotional resilience flourishes.

Practicing Gratitude

The act of gratitude is more than a fleeting thought of thankfulness; it's a sustained practice that reshapes our neural pathways, making us more receptive to joy and contentment. Integrating gratitude into our daily routines can be both simple and profoundly impactful. Consider these methods:

- Gratitude Journaling: Dedicate a few minutes each evening to write down three things you were grateful for that day. These don't have to be grand events; sometimes, the smallest moments hold the most beauty.
- Gratitude Walks: Take regular walks where your sole focus is to observe and internally acknowledge the beauty around you, from the complexity of a leaf to the sun's warmth on your skin.
- Gratitude Reminders: Set random alarms throughout your day as prompts to pause and think of one thing you're grateful for at that moment.

This habitual focus on gratitude can subtly shift our mindset, encouraging us to look for and acknowledge the good in our lives, even on challenging days.

Finding Joy in Small Things

Joy often hides in the nooks and crannies of our everyday lives, waiting to be discovered by those who take the time to look. Learning to notice and savor these moments can significantly enhance our emotional well-being, acting as a buffer against the anxieties and fears that may arise from our attachment patterns. Here are ways to uncover joy in the ordinary:

- Mindful Appreciation: Engage fully with simple pleasures, like the taste of your morning coffee or the feeling of fresh sheets. Allow yourself to be completely absorbed in the experience.
- Creative Expression: Find joy in creativity, whether it's doodling, writing, gardening, or cooking. These activities

aren't about the outcome but the process and the joy it brings.

- Connection with Nature: Nature has a unique way of grounding us and providing perspective. Something as simple as watching birds from a window can be a source of joy and wonder.

By attuning ourselves to the joy present in mundane moments, we cultivate a mindset that values present experiences, enriching our lives with happiness and satisfaction.

Positive Relationships

Our connections with others serve as a fertile ground for joy and gratitude. Positive relationships, marked by mutual respect, understanding, and support, provide a sense of belonging and acceptance, crucial components in our search for emotional resilience. Nurturing these connections involves:

- Active Engagement: Being fully present in your interactions and showing genuine interest in the lives of those you care about fosters deeper connections and shared joy.
- Expressions of Appreciation: Regularly express gratitude towards the people in your life. Letting someone know how much you value their presence can strengthen your bond and bring joy to both parties.
- Shared Experiences: Create opportunities for positive shared experiences, such as meals, walks, or phone calls. These moments become memories that feed your sense of gratitude and joy.

Positive relationships act as mirrors, reflecting the joy and appreciation we offer, creating a cycle of positivity that bolsters our emotional resilience.

Resilience Through Positivity

Cultivating joy and gratitude is not merely an exercise in feeling good; it's a strategic approach to building emotional resilience. Focusing on the positive aspects of our lives creates a buffer against stress and anxiety, making us more capable of navigating the uncertainties and setbacks inherent in life and relationships. This positivity doesn't ignore our challenges but provides a balanced perspective that acknowledges the good and difficulties. Here's how positivity enhances resilience:

- Stress Reduction: Positive emotions help to lower stress levels, offering us clarity and calm in situations that might otherwise overwhelm us.
- Perspective Shift: Focusing on gratitude and joy helps shift our perspective, allowing us to see challenges as manageable and temporary.
- Increased Coping Skills: Fostering a positive outlook strengthens our coping strategies, making us more adaptable and flexible in facing adversity.

In weaving joy and gratitude into the fabric of our lives, we fortify our emotional resilience, ensuring that when storms come, we have the inner resources to weather them. This practice, grounded in the present, acknowledges the beauty in our everyday lives, offering a counterbalance to the anxieties and fears that can cloud our existence. Through gratitude and joy, we find the strength to face our challenges, secure in the knowledge that happiness exists around us, waiting to be acknowledged and embraced.

8.4 CREATING A SELF-CARE RITUAL

Self-care stands out as a beacon of light in emotional healing and resilience, guiding us to where the mind and body can find peace and strength. It's a practice that goes beyond the occasional indulgence, becoming a sacred ritual that nourishes our deepest selves. Through self-care, we give ourselves the love and attention we deserve, reinforcing our worth and ability to overcome anxious attachment patterns that may have shadowed our paths.

Self-Care Importance

The significance of self-care in the process of healing is imperative. It acts as a foundation upon which we can build a stronger, more resilient version of ourselves. When we engage in self-care, we do more than temporarily escape our worries; we address our needs at the most fundamental level, promoting healing from within. This practice becomes exceptionally crucial for those of us navigating the waters of anxious attachment, as it helps to mitigate the stress and anxiety that often accompany this attachment style, grounding us in our worth and capabilities.

Personalized Self-Care Plan

Creating a self-care plan tailored to your unique needs and preferences resembles drawing a map of your journey toward well-being. This plan serves as a guide, helping you navigate through life's challenges with a clear sense of direction and purpose. Here's how you can start crafting your own:

- Identify Your Needs: Begin by taking stock of what aspects of your life require more attention. Is it your physical health, emotional well-being, or spiritual peace? Understanding your needs is the first step in addressing them.

- Choose Your Activities: Select activities that resonate with you and meet your identified needs. These should be practices that you genuinely enjoy and look forward to, ensuring that your self-care plan is one you'll want to stick with.
- Set Realistic Goals: Be realistic about what you can incorporate into your daily or weekly routine. It's better to start small and gradually build up than to set overwhelming goals that become hard to maintain.
- Review and Adjust: Your self-care plan should be a living document that evolves with you. Review it regularly and adjust as needed, ensuring it always aligns with your current needs and circumstances.

Regular Practice

Consistency is key when it comes to self-care. Making it a regular practice ensures that it becomes an integral part of your life rather than an afterthought. To incorporate self-care seamlessly into your routine, consider the following:

- Schedule It: Treat your self-care activities with the same importance as any other commitment. Schedule them into your day or week and honor that time as you would a meeting with someone important.
- Create Rituals: Rituals add a layer of significance to our actions. By creating self-care rituals, you imbue these practices with a sense of sacredness, making them something to look forward to.
- Be Flexible: Life is unpredictable, and flexibility is vital. If your planned self-care activity isn't feasible one day, find a simpler way to honor your commitment to yourself, even

if it's just taking a few deep breaths or enjoying a cup of tea in silence.

Self-Care Activities

The beauty of self-care lies in its diversity; there is no one-size-fits-all approach. Here are some activities to consider, each offering its path to nourishment and peace:

- Meditation and Yoga: These practices combine physical movement, breath control, and meditation to promote inner peace and mindfulness.
- Creative Hobbies: Engaging in creative activities such as painting, writing, or playing music allows for self-expression and can be incredibly therapeutic.
- Nature Outings: Spending time in nature, whether it's a walk in the park or a hike in the woods, can help reduce stress and improve mood, connecting you to the world in a meaningful way.
- Social Outings: While self-care often focuses on solitude, connecting with friends and loved ones can also be a powerful form of self-nourishment, offering laughter, support, and a sense of belonging.

In weaving self-care into the fabric of our daily lives, we enhance our capacity to face life's challenges and deepen our connection to the joy and beauty in our everyday experiences. Through the intentional practice of self-care, we honor our worth, nurture our resilience, and affirm our commitment to a journey of healing and growth.

8.5 EMBRACING CHANGE: THE JOURNEY CONTINUES

Change is the only constant in life, which rings especially true when confronting and working through anxious attachment. Life's inherent fluidity means that we are always on the move, transitioning from one phase to another, learning, unlearning, and relearning. This process can seem daunting, but it has endless opportunities for personal refinement and discovery.

Navigating through life's inevitable changes requires resilience, a quality that, like a muscle, strengthens with use. Here are ways to stand resilient and poised in the face of change:

- Approach change with curiosity. Viewing new situations as opportunities to learn shifts our mindset from one of apprehension to one of exploration.
- Keep an open dialogue with yourself. Regular check-ins on how you feel about changes in your life can help you understand and manage your emotions more effectively.
- Seek support when needed. Turning to friends, family, or professionals can provide perspectives and advice that make adapting to change more manageable.

In overcoming anxious attachment, change is not just inevitable but essential. It signifies growth from old patterns of thought and behavior into new ways of connecting and being. It is a sign that we are moving forward, evolving into versions of ourselves that can form healthier, more fulfilling relationships.

Each step forward is a milestone worth celebrating, no matter how small. These moments of acknowledgment remind us how far we've come and the strength we've garnered. They are not just about congratulating ourselves for enduring the hard times but about recognizing the growth that has emerged from these challenges. Celebrating these milestones can include:

- Sharing your progress with someone who understands and supports your journey.
- Reflecting on where you started and the changes you've noticed in yourself.
- Treating yourself to something that brings you joy as a physical manifestation of your progress.

It's important to remember that the path to overcoming anxious attachment is not linear. It meanders, with its share of ups and downs, successes and setbacks. Each person's path is unique and filled with challenges and victories. However, the opportunity for continuous growth and development remains constant. This process is about more than just managing anxious attachment; it is about enriching our entire being, leading to a more balanced, joyful, and connected life.

In this ongoing adventure, let's hold on to the knowledge that change, while sometimes challenging, brings the promise of new beginnings and fresh perspectives. It allows us to redefine ourselves and our relationships and build a life that resonates with who we are and aspire to be. With every change we encounter, we gain more insight, strength, and a deeper understanding of our capacity to love and be loved securely and freely.

As we move forward, let the essence of change remind us that we are works in progress, beautifully unfinished and constantly evolving. Our journey is one of transformation, a testament to our resilience and enduring hope for more profound connections and a fuller life. This chapter in our story may draw to a close, but the narrative of growth and discovery continues, each page filled with potential and promise.

In closing, we take with us a sense of accomplishment for the strides made, an understanding of the beauty in change, and a readiness for the continued adventure that awaits. As we turn the page, we carry forward the lessons learned, the strength found, and the joy discovered, ready to face what comes next with an open heart and an eager spirit.

cultivating healthy relationships

Picture a garden in full bloom, with an array of flowers and plants thriving side by side. Each species requires a unique blend of sunlight, soil, and water to flourish. Much like gardens, relationships need specific conditions to grow healthy and strong. Recognizing the difference between a garden nurtured with care and one left to wither is the first step in understanding the dynamics of our connections. This chapter aims to guide you through identifying the hallmarks of healthy versus unhealthy relationships, understanding the significance of mutual respect, trust, and support, and navigating the journey from tumultuous to tranquil relational waters.

Recognizing Healthy vs. Unhealthy Relationships

- **Defining Characteristics**

  - Healthy relationships are built on mutual respect, where individuals value each other's opinions, boundaries, and personal space. Trust acts as the

soil that nourishes this growth, allowing partners
to feel secure in their vulnerability. Support,
akin tosunlight, is freely given, empowering each to
pursue their interests and ambitions while
knowing they have a steady base to return to.

- In contrast, unhealthy relationships often lack these
nutrients. Instead of support, there's competition;
instead of trust, suspicion; and instead of respect,
disdain, or neglect.

- **Red Flags**

  - It's crucial to spot the weeds that can strangle a
  relationship. Recognizing early signs of control,
  such as imposing restrictions on who you can
  spend time with or how you dress, disrespectful
  behaviors like belittling comments, and emotional
  manipulation tactics involving guilt or fear to sway
  your decisions, is crucial. These are significant
  warning signs, and promptly identifying them can
  help avoid a lot of emotional distress.

- **Self-Assessment**

  - It's critical to take a step back and assess your role
  in the dynamics of your relationships. This means
  honestly reflecting on how you communicate,
  respecting boundaries, and contributing to the
  overall health of the connection. It's not about self-
  blame but about self-awareness and growth.

- **Transitioning to Health**

  - Moving from an unhealthy to a healthier relationship pattern requires intentional effort. Open communication is the first step, where both individuals can express their needs, fears, and desires without judgment. Setting clear boundaries is another critical step, helping to establish mutual respect and understanding. It's about watering the garden together, ensuring all plants get the nourishment they need to thrive.

Tools for Reflection and Growth

- Checklist of Relationship Nutrients: Create a personal checklist to evaluate the presence of essential nutrients in your relationship: respect, trust, and support. Review it regularly and adjust as needed.
- Journal Prompts for Self-Assessment: Reflect on your contribution to relationship dynamics with guided prompts. For example, "When was the last time I openly communicated my needs?" or "How do I react when my boundaries are challenged?"
- Action Plan for Nurturing Growth: Develop a step-by-step action plan for improving the health of your relationship. Include weekly check-ins with your partner to discuss each other's needs, attend a workshop on communication skills, or set aside time each week to enjoy shared activities that strengthen your bond.
- Resource List: Compile a list of books, articles, podcasts, and counseling services that offer insights and tools for building and maintaining healthy relationships. Keeping

informed and seeking outside perspectives can provide
new strategies for nurturing your relational garden.

Cultivating a healthy relationship is an ongoing process, like
tending to a garden. It requires patience, effort, and a lot of care.
But the rewards—deep connection, mutual respect, and unwavering support—are worth the effort. As you navigate your own
relationship garden, keep these tools in hand, ready to nurture
growth and enjoy the beauty of healthy, flourishing connections.

9.2 THE DANCE OF INDEPENDENCE AND INTIMACY

The interplay between independence and intimacy takes center
stage in the intricate ballet of human relationships. This delicate
balance ensures that both partners experience the freedom to be
their authentic selves while also enjoying the closeness and
connection that intimacy brings. It's about moving together in
harmony, each step a testament to togetherness and individuality.

Maintaining this equilibrium requires conscious effort, as it's easy
for the scales to tip too far in one direction. Too much independence can cause the relationship to feel distant and disconnected.
Too much intimacy and the individual identities may begin to blur,
leading to a loss of self. Striking the right balance allows for a
deeply connected and respectfully autonomous relationship.

Autonomy in Partnership

The quest for autonomy within a relationship is not about creating
distance but nurturing personal growth and self-expression. Here
are strategies to preserve your individuality while fostering a
strong partnership:

- Pursue Personal Interests: Encourage each other to explore hobbies and passions outside the relationship. Pursuing personal interests enriches your life and brings new energy and experiences into the relationship to share with your partner.
- Respect Alone Time: Recognize that time spent apart is not a threat but an opportunity for personal rejuvenation and reflection. It's healthy for partners to enjoy moments of solitude, as it contributes to emotional well-being.
- Maintain Separate Friendships: While shared friends are lovely, maintaining friendships outside the relationship is crucial. These relationships provide additional support networks and perspectives, enriching your life experience.

Intimacy Without Overdependence

Cultivating intimacy without sliding into dependency requires awareness and intention. Consider these approaches to deepen your connection healthily:

- Communicate Openly: Share your thoughts, feelings, and vulnerabilities with your partner. Open communication builds intimacy and trust, allowing both partners to feel seen and understood without fear of judgment.
- Share Experiences: Engaging in activities, from travel to trying out a new hobby, can strengthen your bond. These shared experiences build a reservoir of joy and fond memories that deepen your connection.
- Express Appreciation: Regularly express gratitude and appreciation for each other. Acknowledgment of your partner's qualities and contributions strengthens the emotional bond, reinforcing the value of your connection.

Case Studies

To illustrate the balance between independence and intimacy, consider these real-life examples:

- Case Study 1: Alex and Jamie, a couple who found themselves in a cycle of dependency, sought to reclaim their individual identities. They started scheduling "me" days, where each would pursue personal interests. Jamie joined a local photography club while Alex enrolled in cooking classes. Over time, they noticed a rejuvenation in their relationship, with fresh conversations and increased admiration for each other's passions.
- Case Study 2: Sam and Taylor initially struggled to maintain separate friendships and consciously invested time in individual social circles. They set up weekly outings with friends and encouraged each other to cultivate these external connections. This practice brought new perspectives and experiences into their lives, which they excitedly shared with each other, enriching their relationship.
- Case Study 3: Morgan and Pat discovered that their intimacy was becoming stifling and limiting their personal growth. They decided to implement a routine of open communication, where they would share feelings, dreams, and fears without judgment. This practice deepened their understanding of each other and highlighted the importance of supporting one another's journeys. They learned to grow together by growing individually.

These examples underscore the beauty of navigating independence and intimacy with care and intention. By respecting each other's need for personal space while nurturing a deep emotional connection, couples can create a relationship that thrives on autonomy and closeness. It's a dance of giving and taking, a harmonious blend of togetherness and individuality, that makes the journey of love enriching and fulfilling.

9.3 BUILDING TRUST: THE FOUNDATION OF SECURE ATTACHMENT

Trust is the invisible glue that holds relationships together, silently weaving a tapestry of security and understanding between partners. At its core, trust is built on several key elements: honesty, consistency, and vulnerability. Each aspect creates an environment where love can flourish, free from the shadows of doubt and fear.

- **Trust Building Blocks**

  - Honesty: Think of honesty as truth-telling and an open-book policy between partners. It's about sharing your thoughts, feelings, and intentions transparently, leaving no room for misunderstandings to fester.
  - Consistency: Imagine a steadfast and unwavering lighthouse guiding ships safely to shore. In relationships, consistency serves a similar purpose, offering a reliable beacon for partners amidst the storms of life.
  - Vulnerability: Often mistaken for a sign of weakness, vulnerability is actually a strength. It involves opening your inner world, sharing fears, dreams, and insecurities with your partner, and deepening your connection.

- **Rebuilding Trust**

Rebuilding trust after a betrayal or misunderstanding is akin to mending a broken vase. The cracks might still be visible, but the vase still holds flowers. The process is delicate and requires patience, understanding, and a willingness to forgive.

- Forgiveness: This doesn't mean forgetting or excusing hurtful behavior but instead choosing to release the grip of resentment. It's a gift you give yourself, freeing you from the chains of past pains.
- Open Communication: This involves creating a safe space where both partners can express their feelings and concerns without fear of judgment. It's about listening with empathy, understanding the impact of your actions, and committing to change.
- Trust and Security

Trust is the foundation for a relationship's sense of security. When trust is steadfast, partners feel safe to be authentic and share their hearts without fear of rejection or betrayal. This sense of security is crucial for fostering a secure attachment, where love can grow unimpeded by doubts or fears.

- **Practical Exercises**

For couples looking to build or reinforce trust, consider these practical exercises designed to strengthen your bond.

- Trust Conversations: Set aside time each week to talk about your feelings and any issues affecting your trust in each other. Use this time to practice honesty, listen actively, and show empathy.
- The Trust Fall: While typically seen as a team-building exercise, the trust fall can symbolize reliance and support within a relationship. Taking turns to catch each other

when falling back symbolizes your commitment to being there for one another.

- Secret Swap: Write down a fear or dream you haven't shared with anyone else, and exchange these with your partner. Discussing these secrets can open up new levels of vulnerability and understanding.
- Consistency Calendar: Create a calendar where each of you can mark days with specific actions you've taken to show consistency in your relationship. Review this calendar together at the end of each month to appreciate the effort and reliability each has shown.

In relationships, trust is both the starting point and the destination, a journey that unfolds with each step taken together. Through honesty, consistency, and vulnerability, partners can build a foundation of trust so strong that it becomes the bedrock of a secure attachment. By engaging in exercises that foster openness and reliance, you weave tighter the bonds that connect you, creating a relationship where trust is not just a word but the essence of your connection.

9.4 CELEBRATING DIFFERENCES: NAVIGATING RELATIONSHIP DYNAMICS

In the intricate dance of relationships, partners' differences can be a source of endless fascination or a point of contention. These variations in personality, interests, and perspectives are inevitable and invaluable. They introduce a dynamic richness to relationships, offering endless opportunities for growth, learning, and deeper connection. Recognizing and embracing these differences is foundational to nurturing a vibrant, resilient partnership.

Valuing Differences

Imagine a world where every relationship mirrored the other, conversations flowed in a single tone, and interests never diverged. It might seem harmonious at first glance, but such uniformity would quickly lose its luster, lacking depth and vitality. The truth is differences between partners add color and texture to the relationship tapestry, creating a masterpiece that is far more intriguing and beautiful than any single-threaded work could ever be.

- Strength in Diversity: Partners from different backgrounds or have varying interests bring a wealth of experiences and knowledge into the relationship. This diversity enriches each partner's life and strengthens their bond as they share and learn from one another.
- Growth Opportunities: When we encounter and engage with perspectives that differ from our own, we are challenged to broaden our understanding and empathy. This pushes us out of our comfort zones, fostering personal growth and flexibility.

Understanding vs. Agreement

A common misconception in relationships is that harmony equates to agreement. However, true harmony lies not in unanimous agreement but in understanding and respecting each other's viewpoints, even when they diverge significantly. This understanding fosters a deeper level of intimacy, where both partners feel seen and valued for their authentic selves.

- Empathy as a Bridge: Cultivating empathy allows partners to connect with each other's experiences and emotions, creating a bridge between differing perspectives. It's about hearing and feeling what your partner is expressing, even if you don't share the same view.

- Respectful Dialogue: Maintaining respectful communication is crucial, especially in discussions where opinions differ. You can express your thoughts and feelings while honoring your partner's perspective.

Navigating Conflict

Differences in opinion or preference are natural and expected in any relationship. However, how partners navigate these differences can fortify or fracture their connection. Approaching conflicts with a mindset geared towards understanding and compromise can transform potential rifts into opportunities for strengthening the relationship.

- Seek Common Ground: Instead of focusing on opposing positions, look for underlying values or goals you share. Finding common ground can provide a foundation for resolving conflicts that honor both partners' needs.
- Active Listening: Truly listening to your partner, without planning your rebuttal as they speak, can open up new avenues of understanding. It demonstrates your commitment to valuing their perspective, even when it differs from your own.

Expanding Perspectives

Embracing differences in a relationship encourages both partners to view the world through a wider lens. This openness enriches each individual's life experience and deepens their connection, creating a vibrant, dynamic, and deeply connected partnership.

- Cultivate Curiosity: Approach your partner's interests and perspectives with genuine curiosity. Ask questions, seek to understand, and be open to experiencing the world from their viewpoint.
- Shared Learning: Engage in activities that expose you to new ideas, cultures, or hobbies. This shared journey of discovery can bring a fresh sense of excitement and connection to the relationship.
- Celebrating Uniqueness: Make a conscious effort to celebrate each other's unique qualities and achievements. Acknowledging and appreciating what makes your partner different reinforces their value in your eyes and the relationship.

In navigating a relationship's dynamics, the ability to celebrate differences and view them as opportunities rather than obstacles can transform the way partners relate to each other. It's about building a partnership where diversity is accepted and cherished, understanding trumps agreement, and conflicts are catalysts for growth rather than division. By embracing the unique qualities each person brings to the table, partners can create a relationship that is not only more resilient but also more enriching and fulfilling.

9.5 A NEW BEGINNING: EMBRACING LOVE WITH CONFIDENCE

When we approach love with clarity and purpose, the landscape of our relationships transforms. It's akin to navigating the waters with a compass; knowing where north lies lets us confidently steer our ship, even through uncharted territories. This sense of direction is vital in cultivating love rooted in mutual respect and understanding rather than from insecurity or neediness.

Love with Open Eyes

Loving with open eyes means recognizing the reality of our relationships, including their strengths and challenges, without the veil of idealization or fear. It's about seeing our partners for who they truly are, not who we want them to be or fear they might become. This clear-sighted love fosters a deeper connection, one that's based on truth and acceptance.

- Aware and Intentional Choices: It is crucial to make conscious decisions about who we let into our hearts and lives. Making intentional choices requires a deep understanding of our values, needs, and what we're willing to give and receive in a relationship.
- Acknowledging Imperfections: Embracing the imperfections in ourselves and our partners allows for a more genuine and forgiving relationship. It's understanding that growth is a shared endeavor, with each partner contributing to the journey.

Confidence in Love

The foundation for confidence in love is a secure attachment where trust, respect, and mutual support thrive. This security doesn't happen overnight but results from continuous nurturing and open communication. When we feel secure, our approach to love is marked by optimism and trust, free from past disappointments or fears.

- Optimism and Trust: Stepping into relationships with a belief in positive outcomes sets the tone for how we interact and connect. It's about trusting our partners and our ability to face and resolve challenges as a team.

- Self-assurance: Confidence in love also stems from self-assurance, knowing that we are worthy of love and capable of contributing positively to a relationship. This inner strength guides us through the ups and downs, ensuring our sense of self remains intact.

Starting Fresh

Whether we're venturing into a new relationship or looking to breathe new life into an existing one, starting fresh is about resetting our intentions and expectations. It's a chance to apply the lessons learned from past experiences, paving the way for a relationship that aligns more closely with our desires and values.

- Clear Communication: Communicate your needs, boundaries, and expectations from the outset. This openness fosters a culture of honesty and respect, laying a solid foundation for the relationship.
- Forgiveness and Letting Go: Letting go of past hurts and forgiving ourselves and others frees us from the weight that might hold us back from fully embracing new beginnings.

Celebrating Love

At its core, love is a celebration of connection, growth, and the sheer joy of sharing our life with someone who understands and values us. Remembering to celebrate love in all its forms keeps the spirit of gratitude and joy alive in our relationships.

- Appreciate the Moments: Take time to appreciate both the monumental and the mundane moments. These daily experiences weave the rich tapestry of our shared lives.

- Grow Together: Embrace the journey of growth, both as individuals and as partners. Celebrate the milestones, learn from the setbacks, and keep moving forward together.

As we navigate the complexities of love and relationships, it's crucial to remember that the beauty lies in the journey. It's about more than just finding someone; it's about building something beautiful together that stands the test of time and grows richer with each passing day. In this spirit, we move forward, ready to face the challenges and embrace the joys that come with loving profoundly and confidently.

In this light, our exploration of love and relationships doesn't end here but continues to evolve, enriched by our experiences and the wisdom we gather along the way. Each step is part of a larger journey that shapes us, challenges us, and ultimately brings us closer to the love we seek and deserve.

your feedback is incredibly important to me!

Dear Reader,

Thank you for joining me on this journey through "Overcoming Anxious Attachment." I hope this book has provided you with valuable insights and practical tools to navigate your relationships with greater confidence and emotional freedom.

Your feedback is incredibly important to me, and I would love to hear your thoughts on the book. If you found this book helpful, please consider leaving a review. Your reviews not only help other readers discover this book but also support my work and allow me to continue writing and sharing my knowledge.

Simply scan the QR code below to leave your review:

Warmest regards,

Kelly

conclusion

As we approach the close of our shared journey through the pages of this book, I am reminded of the incredible resilience and courage it takes to confront the roots of anxious attachment and envision a path toward transformation. Together, we've delved into understanding the origins and impacts of anxious attachment —from the foundational theories that give us insight into our emotional world to the practical strategies that offer hope for those seeking change. We've explored the significance of self-awareness, the art of emotional regulation, the power of effective communication, the necessity of setting healthy boundaries, and the development of trust as cornerstones upon which a secure attachment can be built.

It's important to reiterate that transforming anxious attachment into secure attachment is possible and within your reach. The journey from understanding to action, from fear to freedom, is paved with commitment, patience, and practice. You now have the knowledge and tools to embark on this transformative journey of self-discovery and relationship improvement. Remember, the path toward secure attachment is not a destination but a journey of continuous growth and learning.

Our exploration has emphasized a holistic approach to overcoming anxious attachment. Healing encompasses not just the mind but also the body and spirit. Through therapy, self-help techniques, lifestyle changes, and the cultivation of emotional resilience, we've seen how integral physical well-being, mindfulness, self-compassion, and the support of a nurturing community are in this healing process. Your journey towards secure attachment is supported by a foundation that honors all aspects of your being.

Please view this journey not as a task to be completed but as an ongoing process of growth and learning. Stay open to new insights, revisit the strategies outlined in this book as needed, and continue to seek out additional resources and support. Remember, you are not alone on this path. There is a world of support waiting for you, from professionals to communities who understand and share your experiences.

Allow me to offer you a message of hope and empowerment. Your attachment style does not define you. You possess the power to shape your narrative and cultivate the relationships you deserve. This journey is a profound act of self-love and empowerment, a testament to your strength and resilience. Approach each step with patience, kindness, and belief in your capacity for change.

Today, I invite you to take that first courageous step toward transformation. Whether you implement a strategy from our discussions, reach out for professional support, or simply commit to a more mindful and compassionate relationship with yourself, know that each step forward is a step towards emotional freedom and healthier relationships.

Lastly, my heartfelt gratitude goes out to you for allowing me into your world and your willingness to embark on this vulnerable and courageous journey towards secure attachment. It has been an honor to share this exploration with you. Remember, you are embarking on a journey that is not just about overcoming anxious attachment but about rediscovering your essence and unlocking the full potential of your relationships.

Embrace the journey ahead with an open heart and an unwavering belief in your ability to grow, love, and live fully. Here's to new beginnings, the beauty of transformation, and the power of love to heal and connect us all.

references

- *Attachment Theory: Bowlby and Ainsworth's ...* https://www.verywellmind.com/what-is-attachment-theory-2795337
- *Mary Ainsworth Strange Situation Experiment* https://www.simplypsychology.org/mary-ainsworth.html
- *The Neurobiology of Attachment to Nurturing and Abusive ...* https://www.ncbi.nlm.nih.gov/pmc/articles/PMC3774302/
- *How to Move from Anxious Attachment to Secure* https://www.simplypsychology.org/how-to-move-from-anxious-attachment-to-secure.html
- *Infant-parent attachment: Definition, types, antecedents ...* https://www.ncbi.nlm.nih.gov/pmc/articles/PMC2724160/
- *A longitudinal study of maternal attachment and infant ...* https://www.ncbi.nlm.nih.gov/pmc/articles/PMC3796052/
- *Attachment-Based Parenting Interventions and Evidence of ...* https://www.ncbi.nlm.nih.gov/pmc/articles/PMC9622506/
- *Universality claim of attachment theory: Children's ...* https://www.ncbi.nlm.nih.gov/pmc/articles/PMC6233114/
- *Anxious Attachment: How Does It Affect Relationships?* https://www.anxiety.org/anxious-attachment-how-parental-behavior-affects-adult-intimate-relationships
- *Relationship Anxiety: Causes, Signs And How to ... - Forbes* https://www.forbes.com/health/mind/relationship-anxiety/
- *Anxious Attachment in Relationships: 7 Ways To Support Your Partner* https://www.antiloneliness.com/relationships/how-to-support-an-anxiously-attached-partner
- *How to fix an anxious attachment style - Medical News Today* https://www.medicalnewstoday.com/articles/how-to-fix-anxious-attachment-style
- *How to Challenge Negative Self-Talk* https://psychcentral.com/lib/challenging-negative-self-talk
- *What is Mindful Self-Compassion? (Incl. Exercises + PDF)* https://positivepsychology.com/mindful-self-compassion/
- *Physical Health and Insecure Attachment* https://www.attachmentproject.com/attachment-theory/physical-health/#:~:

- *18 Best Self-Esteem Worksheets and Activities (Incl. PDF)* https://positivepsychology.com/self-esteem-worksheets/
- *Attachment Styles and How They Affect Adult Relationships* https://www.helpguide.org/articles/relationships-communication/attachment-and-adult-relationships.htm
- *Cognitive-behavioral therapy for anxiety disorders* https://www.ncbi.nlm.nih.gov/pmc/articles/PMC4610618/
- *Emotional Regulation: Learn Skills To Manage Your ...* https://www.simplypsychology.org/emotional-regulation.html
- *Mindfulness-Based Relationship Enhancement Benefits* https://www.verywellmind.com/understanding-mindfulness-based-relationship-enhancement-4685242
- *7 Ways to Improve Communication in Relationships* https://positivepsychology.com/communication-in-relationships/
- *Setting Healthy Boundaries in Relationships* https://www.helpguide.org/articles/relationships-communication/setting-healthy-boundaries-in-relationships.htm
- *Conflict Resolution in Relationships & Couples: 5 Strategies* https://positivepsychology.com/conflict-resolution-relationships/
- *Deep Listening in Personal Relationships* https://www.psychologytoday.com/us/blog/the-empowerment-diary/201708/deep-listening-in-personal-relationships
- *CBT For Anxious Attachment: Techniques, Benefits And More* https://mantracare.org/therapy/anxiety/cbt-for-anxious-attachment/
- *Insecure Attachments? Emotionally Focused Therapy (EFT ...* https://psychcentral.com/health/eft-therapy
- *19 Best Narrative Therapy Techniques & Worksheets [+PDF]* https://positivepsychology.com/narrative-therapy/
- *Healing Your Anxious Attachment Style: 7 Books to Read* https://www.crackliffe.com/words/2023/09/18/books-to-heal-anxious-attachment
- *What Is Emotional Resilience? (+6 Proven Ways to Build It)* https://positivepsychology.com/emotional-resilience/
- *Mind–Body Approaches to Treating Mental Health Issues* https://www.ncbi.nlm.nih.gov/pmc/articles/PMC4761814/
- *How Gratitude Changes You and Your Brain* https://greatergood.berkeley.edu/article/item/how_gratitude_changes_you_and_your_brain
- *Self-care for anxiety - Mind* https://www.mind.org.uk/information-support/types-of-mental-health-problems/anxiety-and-panic-attacks/self-care/

- *What Does a Healthy Relationship Look Like?* https://www. psychologytoday.com/us/blog/friendship-20/201812/what-does-healthy-relationship-look
- *How to Rebuild Trust After a Betrayal* https://www.healthline.com/health/ how-to-rebuild-trust
- *The Dance Between Intimacy and Independence in Marriage* https://www. gottman.com/blog/dance-intimacy-independence-marriage/
- *How to overcome anxious attachment style - therapist.com* https://therapist. com/relationships/how-to-overcome-anxious-attachment-style/

about the author

Kelly Anne Petty brings a wealth of diverse experiences and a profound passion for healing to her personal work. With a master's degree in counseling, Kelly embarked on a journey in the field of psychotherapy, offering her expertise and compassion in both inpatient and outpatient counseling centers, with a particular focus on addiction treatment. However, her journey didn't stop there. Driven by an innate desire to explore holistic healing modalities, Kelly spent several years working in the tender and profound realm of hospice care. There, she honed her abilities to connect with individuals on a soulful level, witnessing their deeply personal and profound journeys at life's end.

Driven by an insatiable curiosity and thirst for knowledge, Kelly returned to school to become a licensed massage therapist and CranioSacral therapy practitioner. Today, she runs her thriving practice, Rocky Mountain Massage and Bodywork, nestled in the vibrant city of Denver, Colorado. Her hands-on approach to healing, rooted in empathy and understanding, allows her clients to experience profound physical and emotional transformations.

Outside of her professional pursuits, Kelly's life is infused with an unwavering passion for spiritual and personal growth and a deep fascination with metaphysics. She is an avid reader, always exploring new horizons of knowledge and wisdom. Travel is another cornerstone of her life, as she believes in the power of exploration and immersion in different cultures to expand one's understanding of the world.

www.ingramcontent.com/pod-product-compliance
Lightning Source LLC
Chambersburg PA
CBHW032054040426
42335CB00037B/711